North Island Designs 5

A Scrapbook of Sweaters from a Maine Island

North Island Designs 5

A Scrapbook of Sweaters from a Maine Island

Collected by Chellie Pingree

16 New Patterns from

NORTH ISLAND DESIGNS

DOWN EAST BOOKS

Camden, Maine

Photography: Peter Ralston
Graphics and text design: Louis Carrier
Color separations, printing, and binding done in Hong Kong through Four Colour Imports

Library of Congress Catalog Card Number: 92-72725

ISBN   0-89272-322-X

Published by Down East Books,
Camden, Maine 04843

Contents

Welcome

Welcome to the fifth knitting book from North Island Designs. We hope that you will enjoy our new collection of sixteen patterns, which range from simple to complex and from the whimsical to the slightly more serious. All of the sweaters provided in this book were designed by Polly Cabonari, of Montana. Her unique style offers something for everyone.

North Island Designs has been in the business of knitting for ten years. We began on a small farm where my husband, three children, and I were living and farming. There we raised two acres of vegetables, cows, chickens, and a handful of sheep. In the spring, after we sheared the sheep (with hand clippers), I packed the wool into bags and mailed it to Bartlettyarns. Their traditional mill is located in a western Maine town with the wonderful name of Harmony. A few weeks later, three big grain bags stuffed with yarn arrived, and I quickly decided that it was time to either call my knitting neighbors or learn to knit.

I called my neighbors, and although they eventually taught me how to make socks, it was they who started creating—sweaters, socks, hats, wherever their imagination lead them. I added the yarn and their knitted items to my farm stand along with the vegetables, eggs, and rich, creamy milk my customers lined up to buy.

The farm is now long gone, and today we operate North Island Designs out of an old meeting hall in the village, not too far from the island's ferry landing. (Our community, with a winter population of 330, is served by a twelve-car ferry that travels the twelve miles to the mainland twice each day in the winter and three times a day in the summer.) The company has grown from its farm beginnings to a mail-order business that mails over 100,000 catalogs annually and sells knitting books and sweater kits through hundreds of yarn shops across the country.

We hope that you enjoy this collection of patterns, which was put together as a collaborative effort by our crew. Keep knitting, and remember to enjoy the small pleasures of life!

CHOOSING YARNS

This collection of patterns has been designed to be knit using *worsted weight yarn*. Although the samples we show here have been made of wool, you are not bound to this choice of fiber. However, you should use the best quality yarn you can manage, both for comfortable knitting and the most pleasing and durable end results. No matter what your choice of material, it must allow you to meet our *gauge* and *yardage* specifications if your project is to be successful.

To make it easier for you to select your own yarn, we list the quantities used in several ways. First, there is the gauge factor described below: your combination of yarn and needle size *must* match our gauge for accurate results. We show both ounce and yardage (*gram and meter)* measurements because yarn is sold by the ounce, but increasing by yardage is more accurate. This is because many factors influence how much yardage is in a given weight. Specifying "4 oz worsted wt wool" is almost meaningless since some yarns that we use run 180 yards per 4 oz, while others, with no apparent other difference, are a more generous 250 yds for the same weight. Read the yarn labels carefully for this information. If the yardage is not shown, ask the shopkeeper from whom you are buying it. The yarn shop *will* have this information, or you can phone the yarn company and get help from them.

Rest assured that our yarn requirements as listed are generous. Unless you plan to make a garment markedly longer or shorter than ours you will be "safe" with our recommendations! Exact yarn colors and quantities required for each sweater design are given on pages 28 and 29. Sources of the specific yarns we used are listed on page 96.

GAUGE

Our patterns have been plotted using 5 stitches for each horizontal inch, and 7 rows per vertical inch of the body and sleeves (ribbing stitches are worked on smaller needles for a tighter construction). This ratio of stitches and rows per inch is what we mean by gauge—a critical term! For the average knitter, this particular gauge most likely will be reached using size 6 (US) knitting needles, the size we suggest you use for the body and sleeves. We suggest you take a pair of size 6, the required yarn, and cast on 15 stitches. Work 3 inches of stockinette stitch following any section of multicolor work in your pattern. Gently slip the work off the needles and steam press it lightly from the wrong side. Near the top of your swatch, place 2 straight pins directly into the knitting to mark off 2 horizontal inches. *Do not round off the measurements!* Count the number of stitches (include fractions of sts if necessary) in one row between pins. If you have exactly 10, you are in luck and can begin knitting now, but if you don't, here is what to do about it:

MORE THAN 10: This means you knit tighter than our average, which will make your sweater smaller than we indicate. You will have to compensate by knitting with larger needles. Try making another gauge swatch using a size 7 needle and go through the verification steps as before. If you still have too many stitches, do not hesitate to go up in needle size until you reach our gauge, and then use the needle size that works for you, disregarding our size suggestions.

LESS THAN 10: You knit looser than we do, and so your garment will end up larger than ours unless you can produce smaller stitches. This can be done easily by using needles smaller than our size 6 recommendation. You will have to try working a swatch with size 5 or smaller, as necessary until you hit our gauge.

If you change needle size as described above, you will have to adjust the ribbing needle size as well. Go up or down the same number of sizes as you did for the main needles. For example: main needle 7, ribbing needle 5; or main needle 5, ribbing needle 3. Take the time to note these changes on your master pattern!

COLORS

All our patterns have been made in colors of our choosing and then photographed for your easy reference. Feel free to make whatever color changes suit you! Experienced knitters will probably have small amounts of yarn left over from previous projects that could be put to use in these garments, providing they meet the requirements described above. We have used yarns from a number of different sources, and have found that the minor surface and textural differences in the mix have enhanced the overall appearance of our sweaters.

On close examination of the photgraphs, you will see that we have used a variety of yarns, some heathered and some clearly "solid." If used exclusively, heathered yarns tend to produce a somewhat weathered, soft look (see the Farmyard sweater). Keep in mind that, while effective, heathered yarns can appear wishy-washy if there is insufficient contrast among them. Do not be afraid of including fairly dark heathers along with lighter ones; these will simply serve to enliven and clarify the gentle look you are creating.

Alternatively, using clear, solid colors will produce quite different, bolder results. Imagine the Farmyard sweater worked in solid and darker versions of the colors pictured and you will get a good idea of the possibilites facing you! Decide on the look *you* prefer and choose your yarns accordingly.

You must be careful to use yarn of the same dye lot for your main color, since any variations from skein to skein will show up once the yarns are knit. The other colors, however, can be from various dye lots because generally they are used for small discrete areas throughout the garment, and any differences among them will not matter because they will not be viewed side-by-side.

SIZES
Every effort has been made to give you information needed to produce a garment in the size you want. Most people *do* find multicolor knitting somewhat challenging, not for the stitch work (after all, the stitches are the most basic "knit one row, purl one row" routine!), but because the

neccessary color changes often have a real tightening *or* loosening effect on the knitter's tension. Foolish extraneous elements—like your mood!—can also alter your knitting. These variations and the potential for the problems they can cause are why we are so insistent that you make every effort to meet the gauge! Fortunately, most of these irregularities can literally be ironed out when you steam your work prior to sewing it up, so do not panic if you are occasionally a bit off.

To select the pattern size likely to produce the results you want, measure a worsted-weight sweater that fits the way you like. Compare these measurements to ours to narrow down your choice of size.

To increase body and sleeve length, add a few rows in ribbing and a couple of rows in stockinette stitch above ribbing in same ribbing color.

To decrease sleeve length, reduce ribbing by a few rows and delete rows only at solid-color rows between motifs.

Should you want a bigger sweater than we allow for in the pattern, simply increasing 2 sts on either side of both front and back will make the sweater a size 42, adding 4 sts will make the sweater a size 44, etc. You will need to increase sleeve sts accordingly. Remember that you will need more yardage of your main-color yarn.

NEEDLE CONVERSION CHART

American	Canadian	Metric
0	14	2
1	13	2.5
2	11	3
3	10	3
4	9	3.5
5	8	4
6	7	4.5

Kathy's heading off to teach knitting class.

Monica taking a relaxing break from her springtime chores.

Fox Hunt

Hannah awaits the ferry bringing her summer friends back after a long winter.

12

Monica's already picking out holiday gifts.

Allison checking out the orchard in early spring.

Monica's ready for a day of sailing around the island.

Laura's ready for her first whale-watching excursion on Penobscot Bay.

Foxberry

Here's Christie posing for yet another North Island Designs photo.

Kathy's contemplating where that first trout is waiting to be caught.

Wendy's off to picnic on her favorite beach at Mullen's Head Park.

Monica's waiting for the rest of the gang to arrive to set up camp.

Oh, how Robin loves her flower gardens.

Scallop Shells

Caroline's waiting to see what the catch of the day is.

Fall Fruit

Allison's picking out the flowers for her garden.

Caroline had a beautiful day for a quick trip to the mainland.

Paula enjoying some time by the ocean before going back to work.

SIZES

Bust Measurement:	36"	38"	40"
	91.5 cm	96.5 cm	101.5 cm
Finished Size:	38"	40"	42"
	96.5 cm	101.5 cm	106.5cm
Underarm Body L:	14"	14"	14"
	35.5 cm	35.5 cm	35.5 cm
Armhole Depth:	7½"	7¾"	8"
	19 cm	19.5cm	20 cm
Underarm Sleeve L:	17¼"	17¼"	17¼"
	44 cm	44 cm	44 cm

SUPPLIES

Worsted weight yarn (see pages 27–29 for specific requirements); single-point US knitting needles, sizes 4 and 6 or as needed to reach suggested gauge of 5 sts and 7 rows per inch; 16"/40.5 cm circular #5 needle; assorted bobbins; tapestry needle; straight pins.

Note: most knitters will find it helpful to go over the chart, outlining their size grid with a fine-line colored marker. This simple step will visibly define the correct stitches to follow. In addition, it is a good idea to tape snips of the colored yarn you will be using right next to their symbol on the chart. Note that graphs as originally charted are to be read from right to left for right-side (knit) rows, and from left to right for wrong-side (purl) rows. Any changes you make to the length of sleeve or body may affect this order.

BACK

RIBBING: With smaller needles and color indicated, CO 84 (88, 92) sts. Establish a k1, p1 ribbing across first row. On subsequent rows, knit the knit stitches and purl the purl stitches until ribbing measures 2½"/6.5 cm or desired depth.

BODY: Change to larger needles and purl, increasing 8 sts evenly across row. This estab-lishes your wrong side, and gets you to 92 (96, 100) sts.

Study your chart carefully to see which method of colorwork you will use. Most of the charts are done in the intarsia method. This means using a separate bobbin for each major color area of the design instead of carrying strands across the back of the work from one area to the next. This way, the knitted fabric will lay flat and not pucker, which can happen when many strands of yarn are carried behind. (You may want to attach more than one ball of main color in some areas.) Since the re-sulting fabric is only one layer thick, intarsia knitting also yields a less bulky fabric and uses less yarn. The all-over background patterns are worked as regular multicolor knitting, however, not as intarsia.

Follow chart to armhole, remembering to use only the small background motifs and not the primary front design.

ARMHOLE: BO 3 sts at start of next 2 rows. To shape curve of armhole, BO 1 st at start of next 8 rows. Do this by sl 1, work 1, psso to ensure that selvedge will be smooth when it is time to sew the sleeve in! 78 (82, 86) sts rem. Follow chart straight up until you reach NECK and SHOULDER shaping.

At start of next 2 rows, BO 10 (12, 14) sts. (Note: to make as smooth a seam line as possible and to avoid leaving a step where you make the first decreases, sl 1, work 1, and psso, then BO rem sts as usual. Start all decreases this way.) At beg. of next row, BO 8 sts; work 8; BO center 26 sts loosely, purlwise; work to end of row. Complete one shoulder or attach another ball of same yarn to other side of neck so you can work both shoulders simultaneously, following chart to complete all neck and shoulder shapings.

FRONT

Set up as for back, except now you will work *all*

the designs on your chart. Decide on your approach for each section before you attempt to work it! Follow chart as is until it is time to begin neck shaping.

Work across 32 (34, 36) sts. BO center 14 sts; work to end of row. You can work one shoulder at a time or complete both shoulders at the same time by attaching another ball of the necessary yarn(s) to other shoulder.

SLEEVES

CUFFS: With smaller needles and color indicated, CO 40 (44, 48) sts. Work in k1, p1 ribbing for 3½"/9 cm or as desired. Change to larger needles and p across row, increasing 8 sts. This marks your wrong-side row and gives you 48 (52, 56) sts. Follow chart, beginning with a k row, and make any desired adjustments to length.

INCREASES may be worked in any number of ways, but for the smoothest seam line (and so, the easiest sewing), we suggest that you work the first st of an inc row as usual, then make the increase by knitting the loop that lies between it and the second st. Work to last st; knit the loop that lies between it and the st before; knit the last st (2 increases made). Keep these sts in the correct color sequence.

When you reach the DECREASES for the sleeve cap, remember to work them as you did for the armholes on front and back.

At this point, work in any loose ends of yarn and lightly steam all 4 pieces, making sure that their dimensions are correct and that stitches lie smoothly. You will find that steam really does help in this! Selvedges also need to be good and flat if you are to be able to sew the seams properly.

SHOULDER SEAMS

With right sides of work together, carefully backstitch shoulder seams. If you pressed the selvedges carefully as suggested above, you will have no problem making the desired smooth, non-bulky seam.

NECK RIBBING

With circular needle and ribbing yarn (right side of work facing you), pick up 26 sts from back of neck, 25 (27, 29) sts from along left neck, 14 from front throat area, and 25 (27, 29) sts along right neck edge, for a total of 90 (94, 98) sts. Work k1, p1 ribbing for 1"/2.5 cm, then bind off in ribbing (that is, knit the knits and purl the purls before you bind them off) to ensure maximum elasticity.

FINISHING

Mark the center of the top of the sleeve caps, and pin that point to the shoulder seams, right sides together. Pin remainder of sleeve cap to armhole, easing as necessary to prevent unnecessary puckers or gathers. For best results, sew from shoulder seam down one side of the sleeve cap and then down the other side, using a loose but firm backstitch. Sew up body seams, then down sleeve seams. Again, bury ends of yarn well and give garment its final steaming.

ABBREVIATIONS

BO: bind off
CO: cast on
DEC: decrease
INC: increase
PSSO: pass the previously slipped st over the next one worked
REM: remain; remaining
SL 1: with right-hand needle, enter first st on left-hand needle as if to purl, transferring it to right-hand needle without working it.
ST: stitch
ST ST: stockinette stitch.

WILDERNESS

6 4-oz. sk (1,200 yds/ *1097 m*) Lt. Blue Heather
200 yds/ *183 m* Navy
100 yds/ *91 m* Med. Pink Heather
100 yds/ *91 m* Wine
50 yds/ *45 m* Natural
50 yds/ *45 m* Black
50 yds/ *45 m* Dk. Green Heather

FARMYARD SAMPLER

4 4-oz sk (630 yds/ *567 m*) Oatmeal
210 yds/ *192 m* Natural
150 yds/ *137 m* Lt. Blue Heather
150 yds/ *137 m* Lt. Green Heather
100 yds/ *91 m* Dk. Green Heather
75 yds/ *68.5 m* Yellow
75 yds/ *68.5 m* Tan
75 yds/ *68.5 m* Olive Green
50 yds/ *45 m* Blue Gray
50 yds/ *45 m* Lt Pink Heather
50 yds/ *45 m* Dk. Brown
25 yds/ *22.5 m* Med. Pink Heather
25 yds/ *22.5 m* Golden Brown

FOX HUNT

6 4-oz sk (1050 yds/ *960 m*) Dk. Green
260 yds/ *237 m* Oatmeal
100 yds/ *91 m* Rust
75 yds/ *68.5 m* Blue Gray
75 yds/ *68.5 m* Natural
50 yds/ *45 m* Maroon Heather
30 yds/ *27 m* Gray Brown/Natural
30 yds/ *27 m* Med. Gray
30 yds/ *27 m* Tan
25 yds/ *22.5 m* Wine
20 yds/ *18 m* Lt. Green Heather
20 yds/ *18 m* Dk. Brown Heather
15 yds/ *13.5 m* Gold

SLEIGH RIDE

6 4-oz sk (1050 yds/ *960 m*) Purple
420 yds/ *384 m* Natural
40 yds/ *36.5 m* Maroon Heather
30 yds/ *27 m* Dk. Green
30 yds/ *27 m* Tan
15 yds/ *13.5 m* Lt. Blue Heather
15 yds/ *13.5 m* Dk. Green Heather
15 yds/ *13.5 m* Med. Pink Heather
15 yds/ *13.5 m* Gold
15 yds/ *13.5 m* Dk. Brown
10 yds/ *9 m* Navy
10 yds/ *9 m* Lt. Pink Heather

COUNTRY APPLES

6 4-oz sk (1,200 yds/ *1097 m*) Natural
100 yds/ *91 m* Teal
100 yds/ *91 m* Red Plum Tweed
100 yds/ *91 m* Med. Blue Tweed
75 yds/ *68.5 m* Lt. Pink Tweed
50 yds/ *45 m* Dk. Brown

SAILING

6 4-oz sk (1,150 yds/ *1051 m*) Navy Blue
95 yds/ *87 m* Lt. Blue
95 yds/ *87 m* White
50 yds/ *45 m* Red

WHALE

6 4-oz sk (1,200 yds/ *1097 m*) Med. Blue Tweed
200 yds/ *192 m* Natural
50 yds/ *45 m* Navy
25 yds/ *22.5 m* Teal

FOXBERRY

6 4-oz sk (1,200 yds/ *1097 m*) Lt. Green
        Heather
100 yds/ *91 m* Med. Brown Heather
50 yds/ *45 m* Dk. Brown Heather
50 yds/ *45.m* Oatmeal
50 yds/ *45 m* Dk. Green
50 yds/ *45 m* Dk. Blue Tweed

WILY TROUT

6 4-oz sk (1,200 yds/ *1097 m*) Oatmeal
210 yds/ *192 m* Lt. Green Heather
50 yds/ *45 m* Purple Tweed
25 yds/ *22.5 m* Dk. Brown
25 yds/ *22.5 m* Lt. Blue Green
20 yds/ *18 m* Pink Heather
20 yds/ *18 m* Red Plum Tweed
20 yds/ *18 m* Dk. Green
20 yds/ *18 m* Med. Green

REINDEER

6 4-oz sk (1,150 yds/ *1051 m*) Beige
190 yds/ *174 m* White
95 yds/ *87 m* Dk. Red
95 yds/ *87 m* Dk. Green
10 yds/ *9 m* Brown

WINTER BEARS

6 4-oz sk (1,200 yds/ *1097 m*) Blue Gray
210 yds/ *192 m* Natural
100 yds/ *91 m* Oatmeal
75 yds/ *68.5 m* Dk. Green Heather
50 yds/ *45 m* Maroon Heather
50 yds/ *45 m* Med. Brown Heather
50 yds/ *45 m* Dk. Brown

FLOWER GARDEN

6 4-oz sk (1,200yds/ *1097m*)Lavender
        Heather
210 yds/ *192 m* Dk. Green Heather
80 yds/ *73 m* Lt. Green Heather

50 yds/ *45 m* Purple Tweed
50 yds/ *45 m* Dk. Blue Tweed
25 yds/ *22.5 m* Lt. Blue Heather
20 yds/ *18 m* Med. Gray Tweed
10 yds/ *9 m* Yellow

SCALLOP SHELLS

6 4-oz sk (1140 yds/ *1026 m*) Lt. Blue
285 yds/ *261 m* White
285 yds/ *261 m* Pink

FALL FRUIT

6 4-oz sk (1,200 yds/ *1097 m*) Blush
70 yds/ *64 m* Med. Pink Heather
70 yds/ *64 m* Red Plum Tweed
50 yds/ *45 m* Purple Tweed
50 yds/ *45 m* Dk. Green
35 yds/ *32 m* Med. Green Heather
35 yds/ *32 m* Purple
30 yds/ *27.5 m* Lt. Pink Tweed
25 yds/ *22.5 m* Lt. Green Heather
25 yds/ *22.5 m* Red Grape

COYOTE

6 4-oz sk (1,200 yds/ *1097 m*) Natural
200 yds/ *183 m* Tan
100 yds/ *90 m* Teal
100 yds/ *90 m* Hot Pink
10 yds/ *9 m* Bright Yellow
10 yds/ *9 m* Orange
10 yds/ *9 m* Red

QUILTED GOOSE

5 4-oz sk (1000 yds/ *917 m*) Natural
260 yds/ *238 m* Dk. Blue Tweed
100 yds/ *90 m* Dk Green Heather
100 yds/ *90 m* Lt. Blue Green
25 yds/ *22.5 m* Gray Brown
25 yds/ *22.5 m* Black
15 yds/ *13.5 m* Lt. Gray

Upper Body Chart

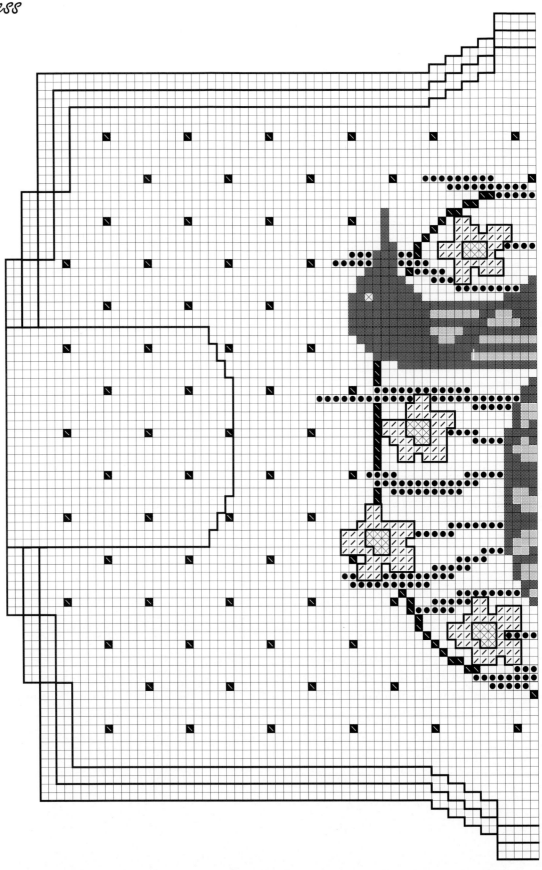

Lower Body Chart

Ribbing Color: Blue Heather

	Lt. Blue Heather		Black		Med. Pink Heather	●	Dk. Green Heather
◼	Navy		Natural	⊠	Wine		

36 38 40

40 38 36

31

Wilderness

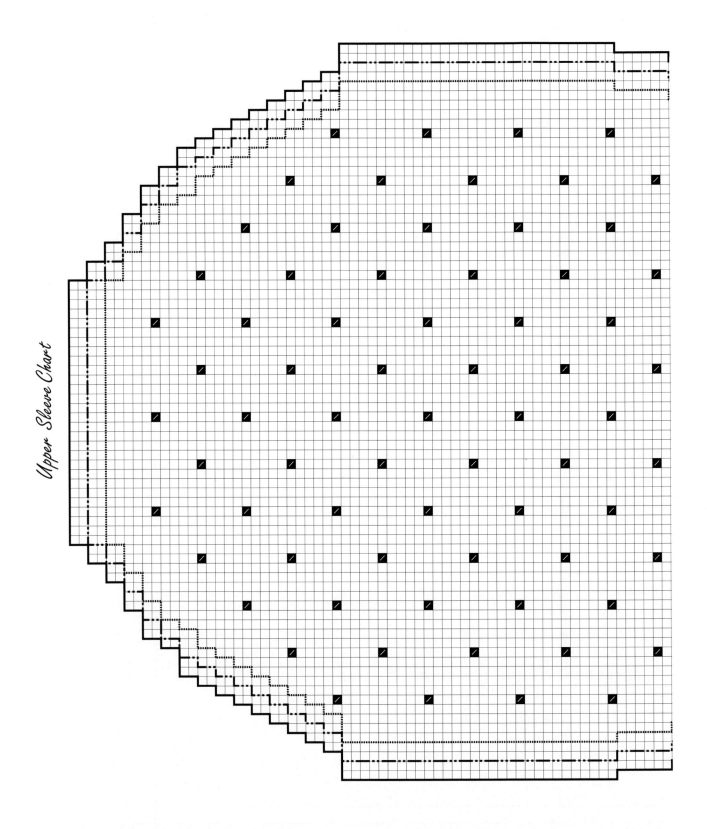

Upper Sleeve Chart

Lower Sleeve Chart

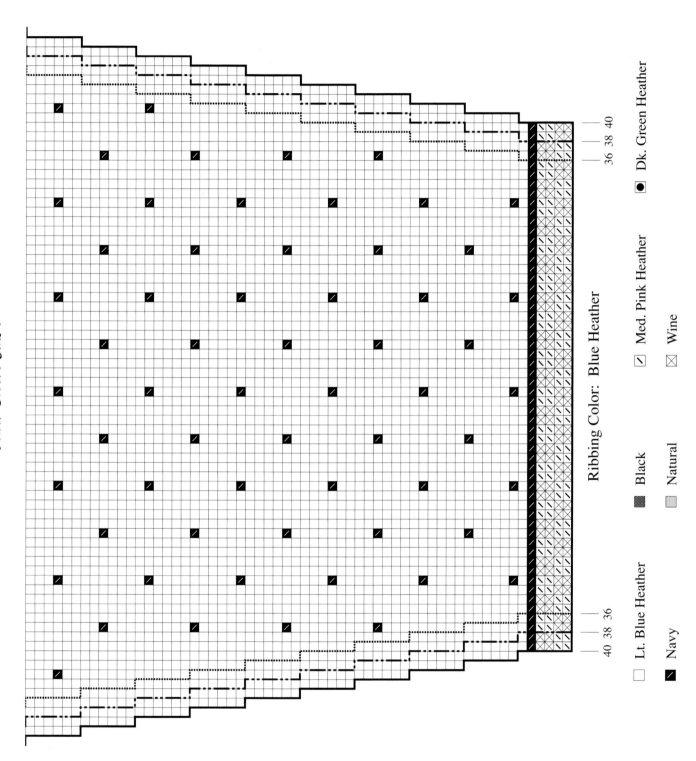

Ribbing Color: Blue Heather

☐ Lt. Blue Heather   ▨ Black   ◩ Med. Pink Heather   ● Dk. Green Heather

▨ Navy   ▨ Natural   ⊠ Wine

Upper Body Chart

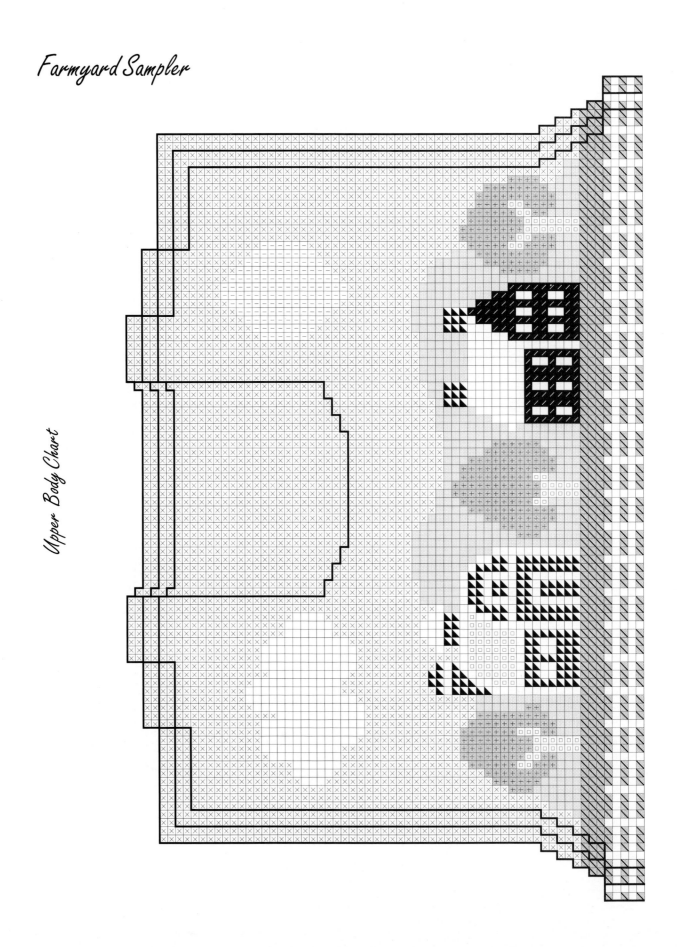

Lower Body Chart

Ribbing Color: Oatmeal

▦ Oatmeal (MC)	◪ Tan	◹ Golden Brown	◩ Olive Green
⊠ Lt. Blue Heather	◣ Med. Pink Heather	⊞ Dk. Green Heather	⊟ Lt. Green Heather
☐ Natural	☐ Dk. Brown	● Blue Gray	— Yellow
		◁ Lt. Pink Heather	

35

Upper Sleeve Chart

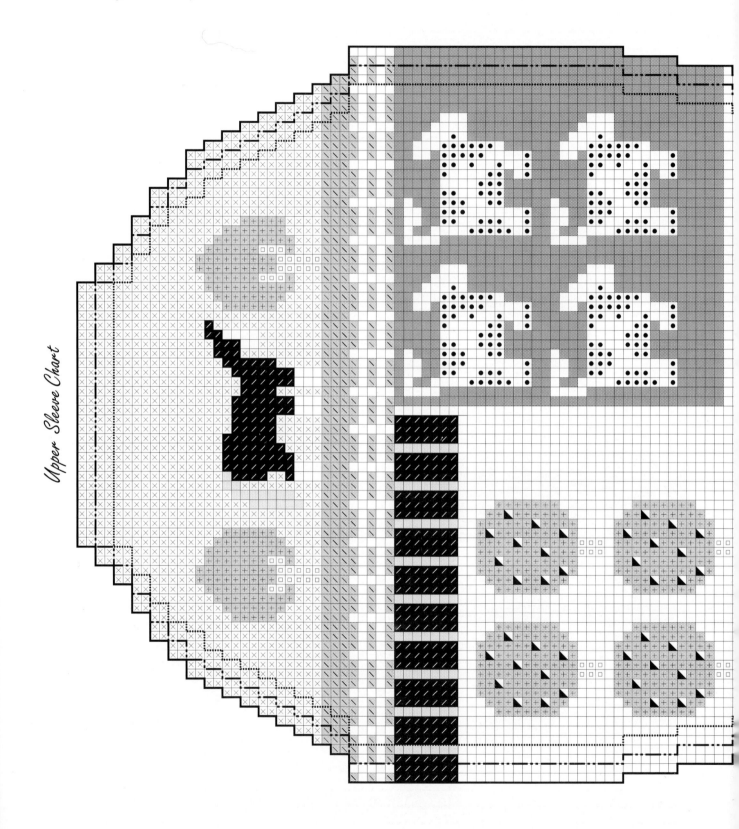

Lower Sleeve Chart

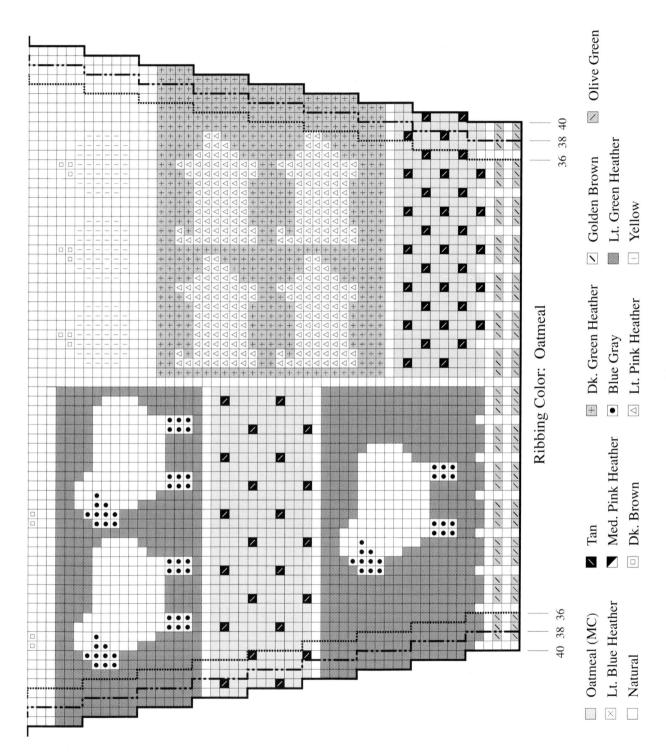

Ribbing Color: Oatmeal

▦ Oatmeal (MC)	▨ Tan	⊞ Dk. Green Heather	⧄ Golden Brown	▨ Olive Green
⊠ Lt. Blue Heather	◣ Med. Pink Heather	● Blue Gray	⬚ Lt. Green Heather
▢ Natural	▢ Dk. Brown	◁ Lt. Pink Heather	⊟ Yellow

Upper Body Chart

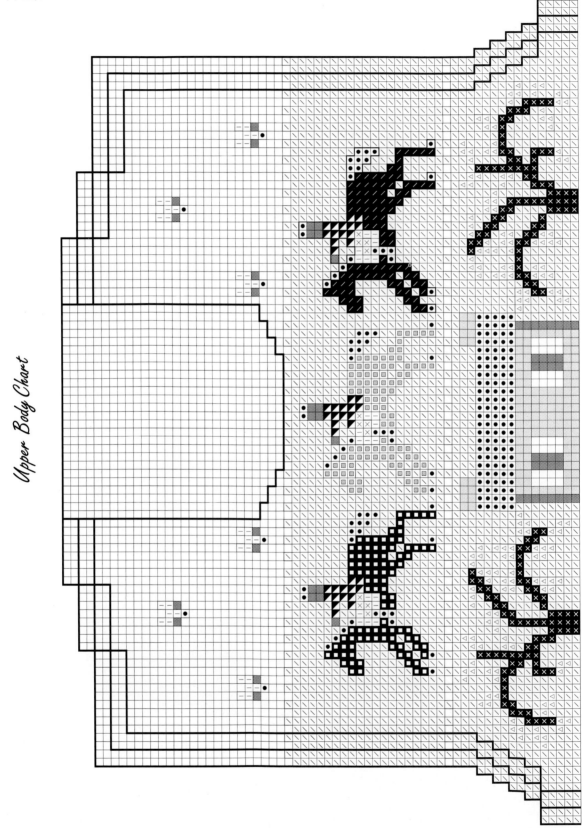

Lower Body Chart

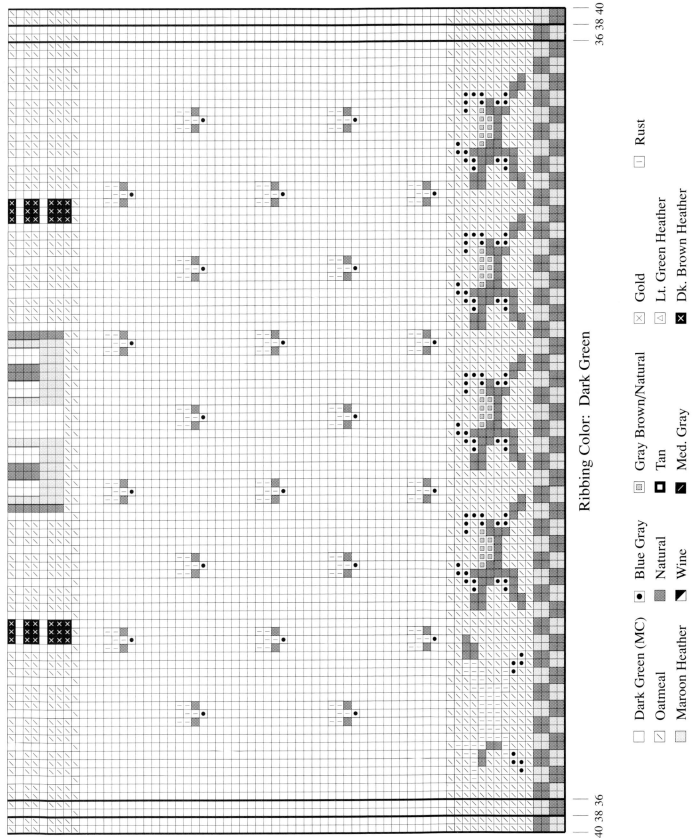

Ribbing Color: Dark Green

☐ Dark Green (MC)	● Blue Gray	▦ Gray Brown/Natural	☒ Gold	☐ Rust
⊘ Oatmeal	▦ Natural	☐ Tan	◁ Lt. Green Heather	
▦ Maroon Heather	◣ Wine	◣ Med. Gray	☒ Dk. Brown Heather	

Fox Hunt

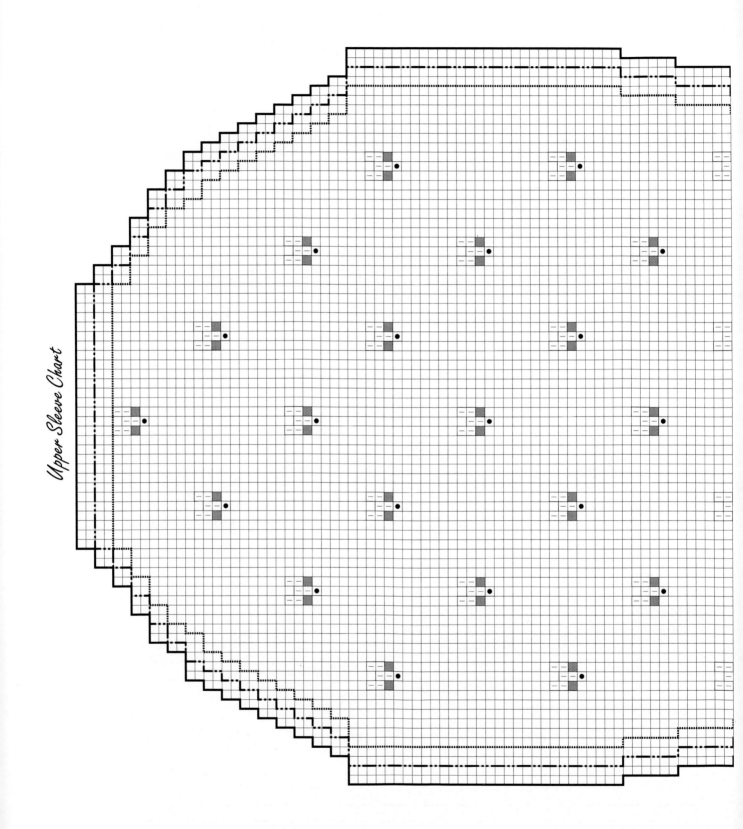

Fox Hunt

Lower Sleeve Chart

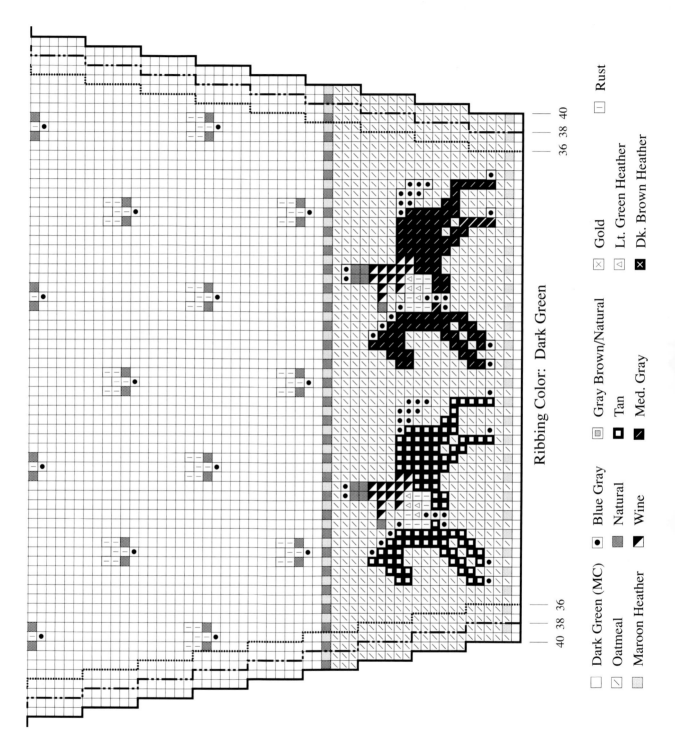

Ribbing Color: Dark Green

□	Dark Green (MC)	•	Blue Gray
▨	Gray Brown/Natural	⊠	Gold
▧	Oatmeal	▨	Natural
◨	Tan	△	Lt. Green Heather
▨	Maroon Heather	◨	Wine
▨	Med. Gray	✕	Dk. Brown Heather
□	Rust		

40 38 36   36 38 40

41

Upper Body Chart

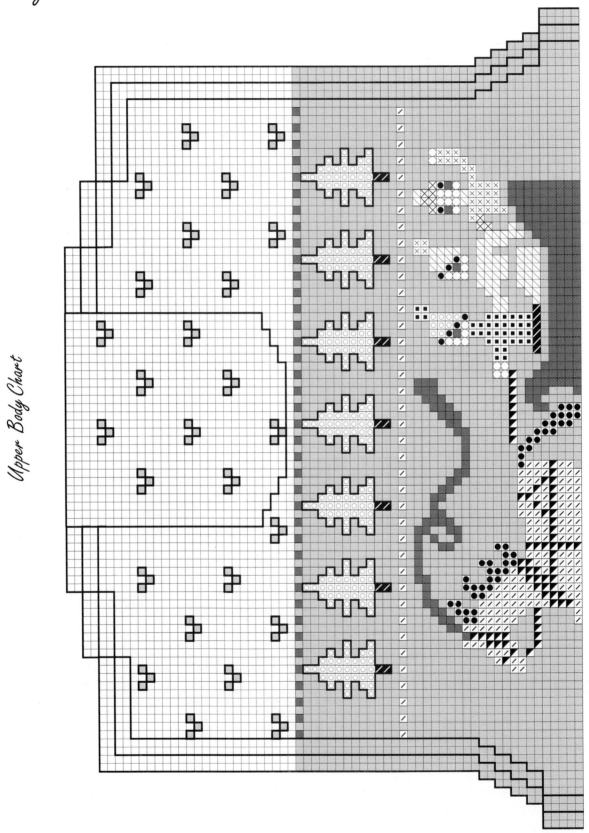

Lower Body Chart

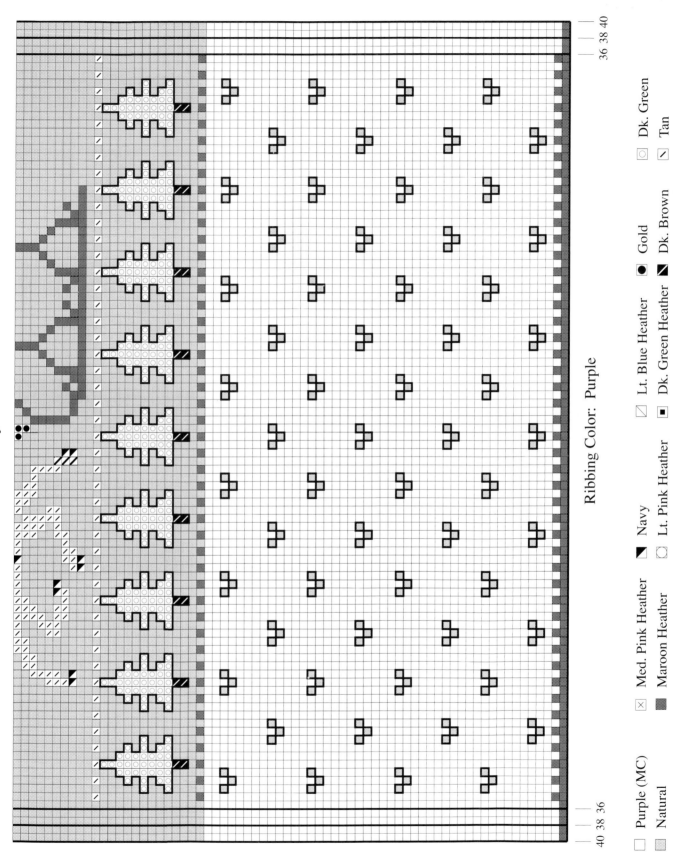

40 38 36

36 38 40

Ribbing Color: Purple

Purple (MC)

Natural

☒ Med. Pink Heather

▧ Maroon Heather

◣ Navy

◯ Lt. Pink Heather

◪ Lt. Blue Heather

◪ Dk. Green Heather

● Gold

■ Dk. Brown

◩ Dk. Green

◹ Tan

43

Sleigh Ride

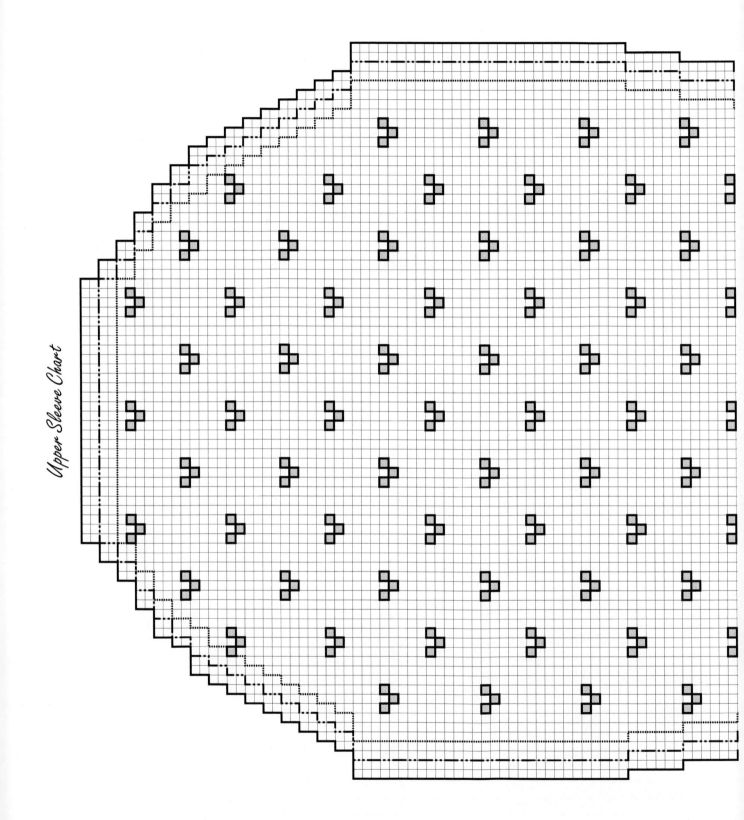

Upper Sleeve Chart

44

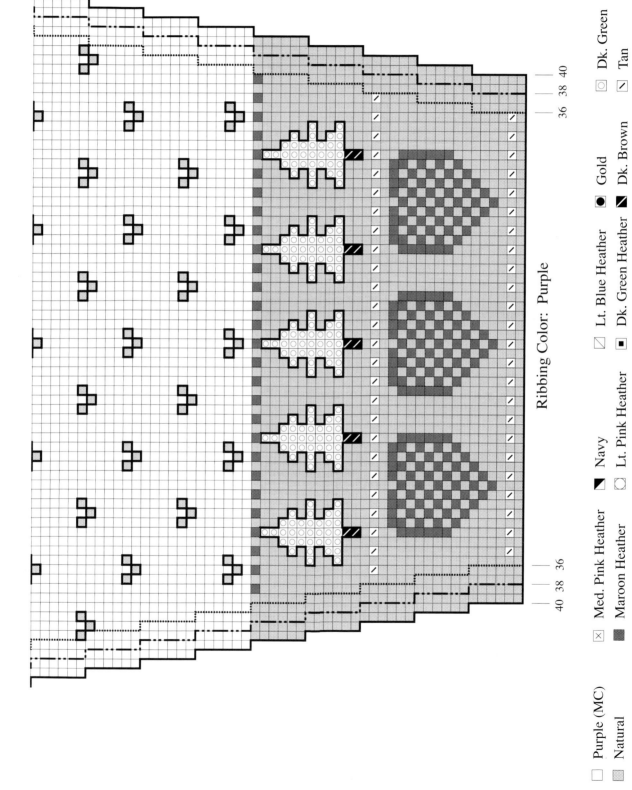

Lower Sleeve Chart

Ribbing Color: Purple

☐ Purple (MC)	⊠ Med. Pink Heather	◢ Navy	⬚ Lt. Blue Heather	● Gold	◐ Dk. Green
▨ Natural	▦ Maroon Heather	◯ Lt. Pink Heather	▨ Dk. Green Heather	◣ Dk. Brown	⬚ Tan

Upper Body Chart

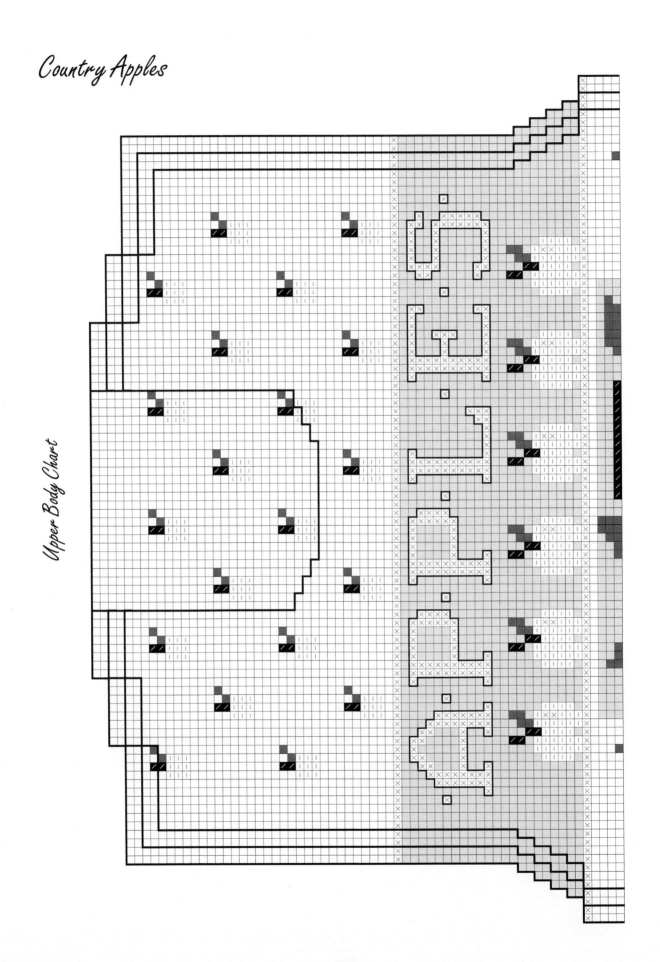

46

Lower Body Chart

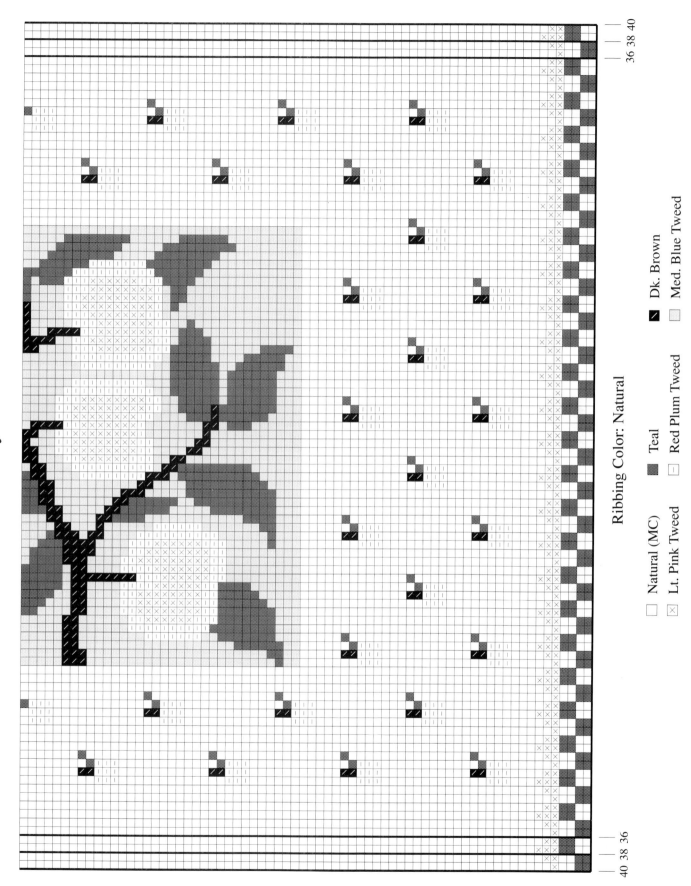

36 38 40

36 38 40

40 38 36

40 38 36

Ribbing Color: Natural

☐ Natural (MC)   ■ Teal   ◼ Dk. Brown

☒ Lt. Pink Tweed   ⊟ Red Plum Tweed   ▨ Med. Blue Tweed

Country Apples

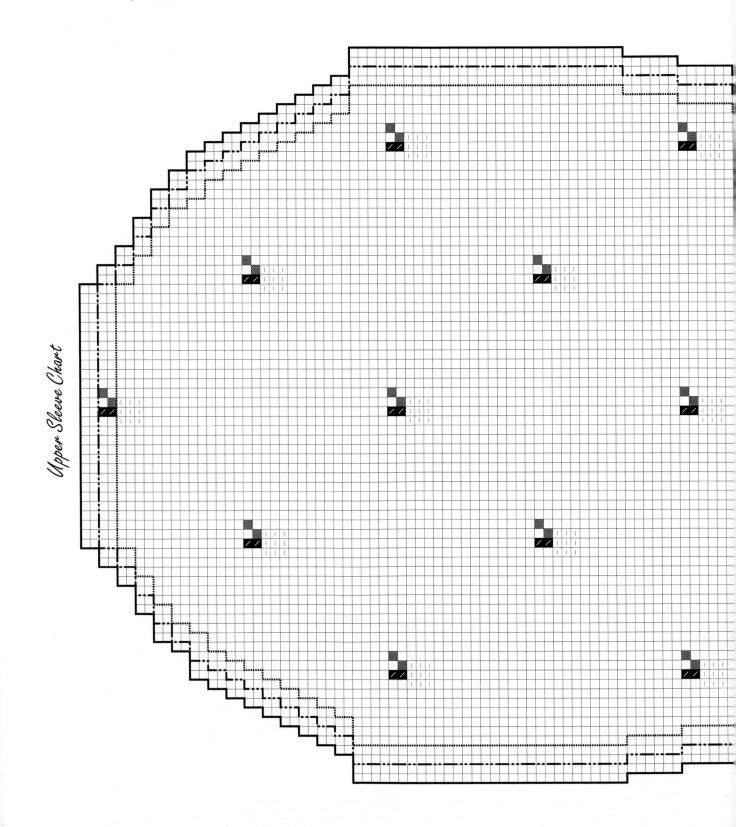

Upper Sleeve Chart

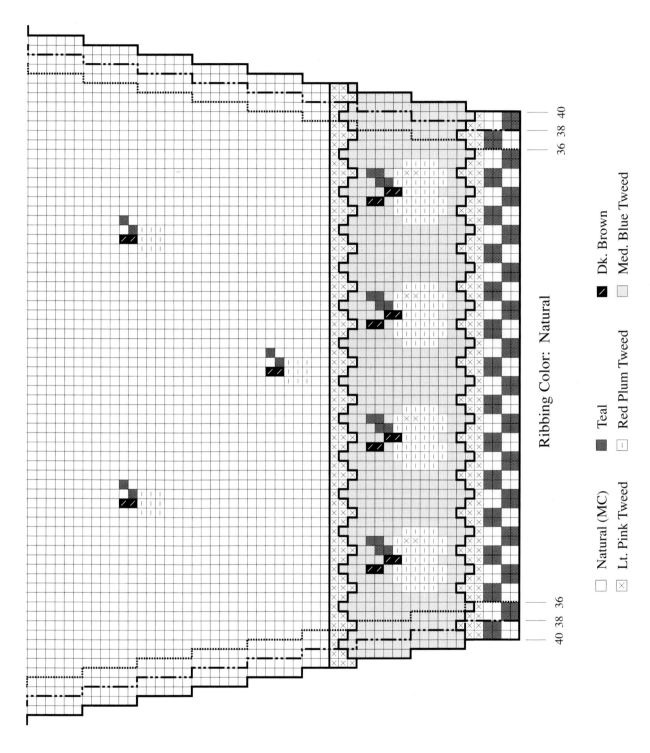

Lower Sleeve Chart

Ribbing Color: Natural

☐ Natural (MC)	◼ Teal
☒ Lt. Pink Tweed	⊟ Red Plum Tweed
◼ Dk. Brown	▨ Med. Blue Tweed

36 38 40

40 38 36

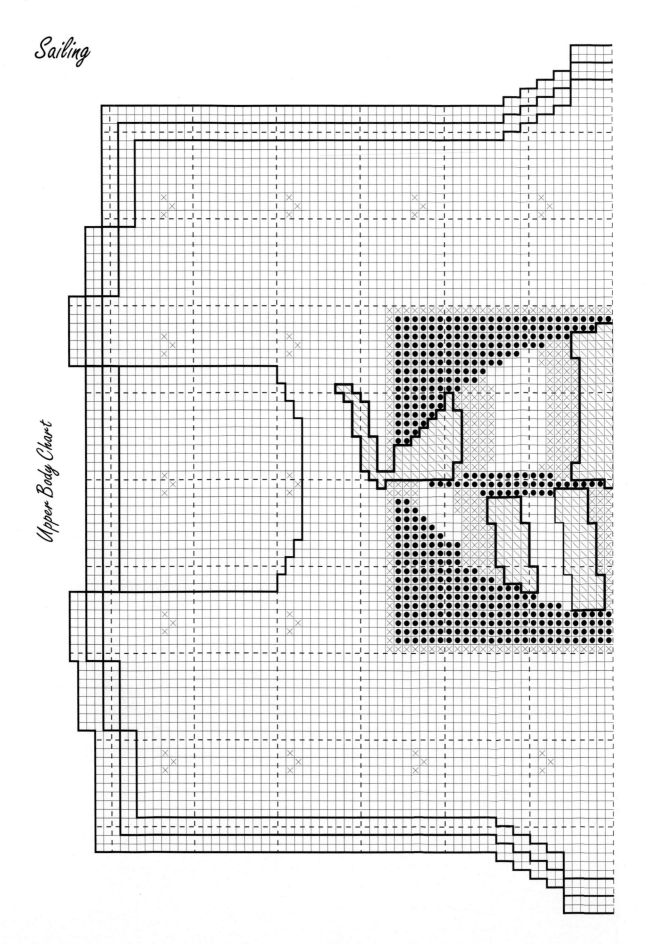

Upper Body Chart

Lower Body Chart

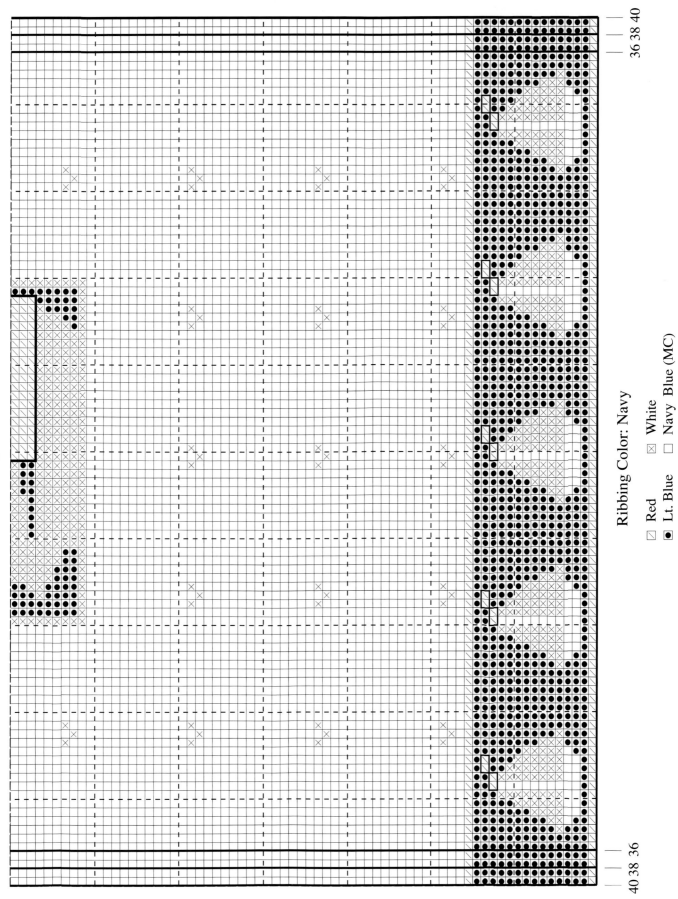

36 38 40

36 38 40

40 38 36

40 38 36

Ribbing Color: Navy

⊠ Red   ⊠ White

● Lt. Blue   ☐ Navy Blue (MC)

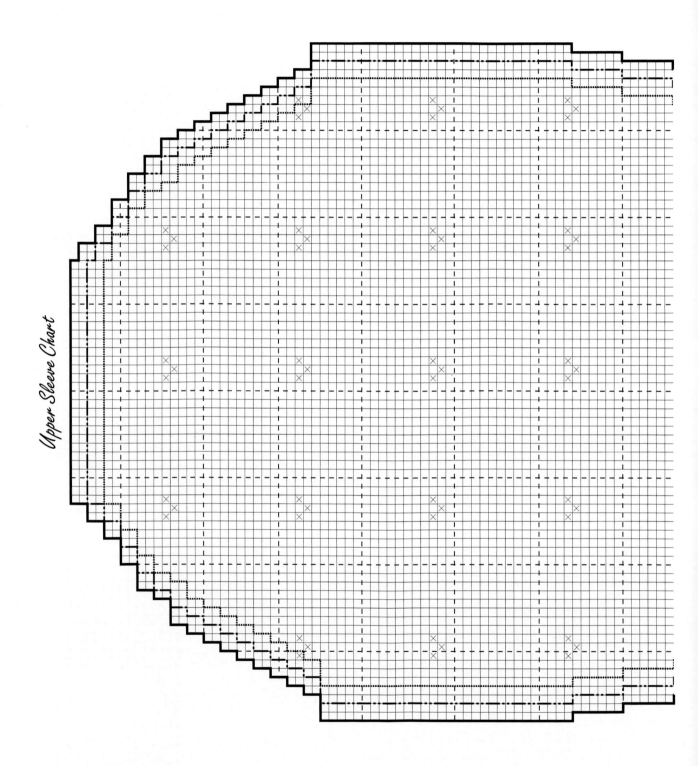

Upper Sleeve Chart

Lower Sleeve Chart

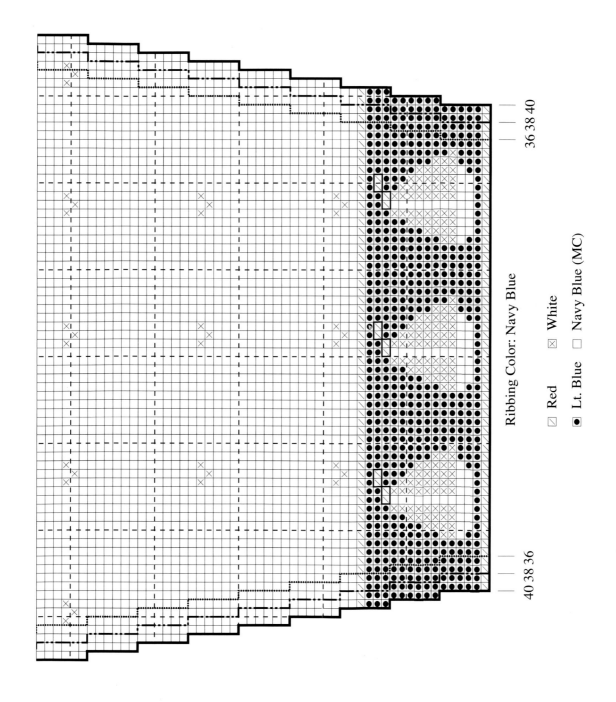

36 38 40

40 38 36

Ribbing Color: Navy Blue

▨ Red ⊠ White

● Lt. Blue ☐ Navy Blue (MC)

Whale

Upper Body Chart

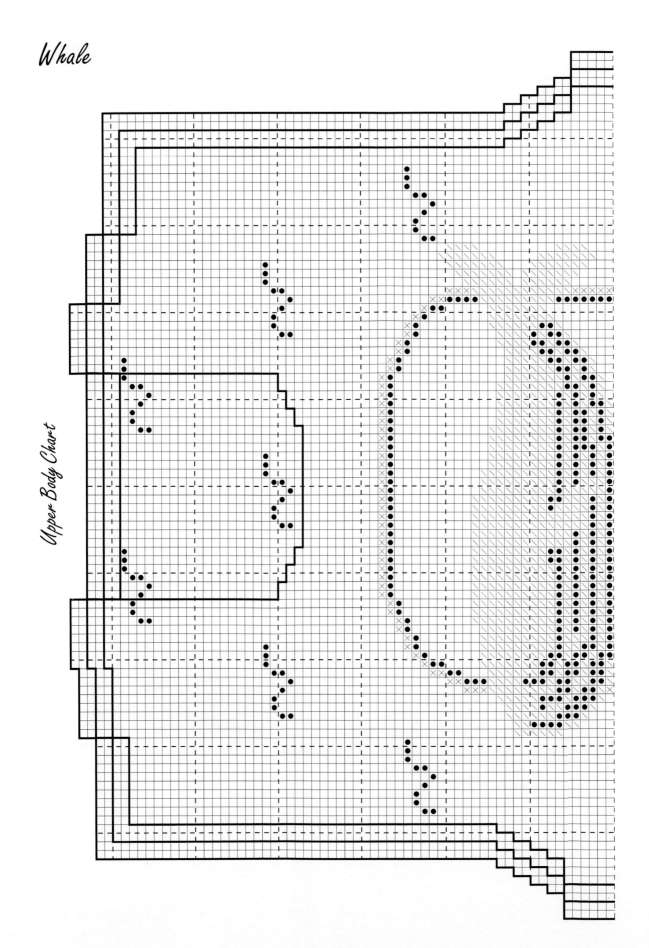

Lower Body Chart

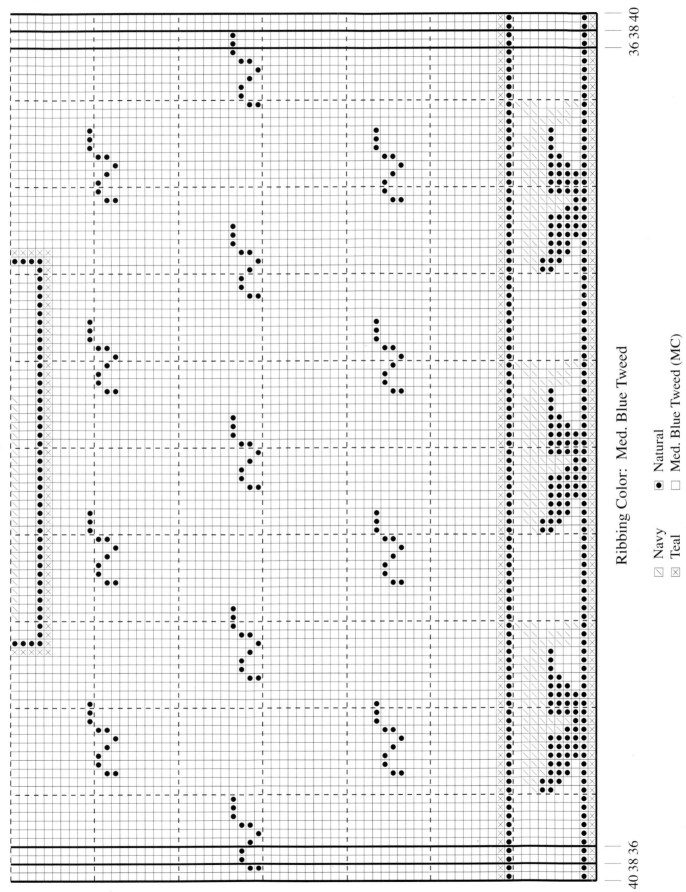

36 38 40

36 38 40

Ribbing Color: Med. Blue Tweed

☑ Navy   ● Natural
☒ Teal   ☐ Med. Blue Tweed (MC)

40 38 36

40 38 36

Whale

Upper Sleeve Chart

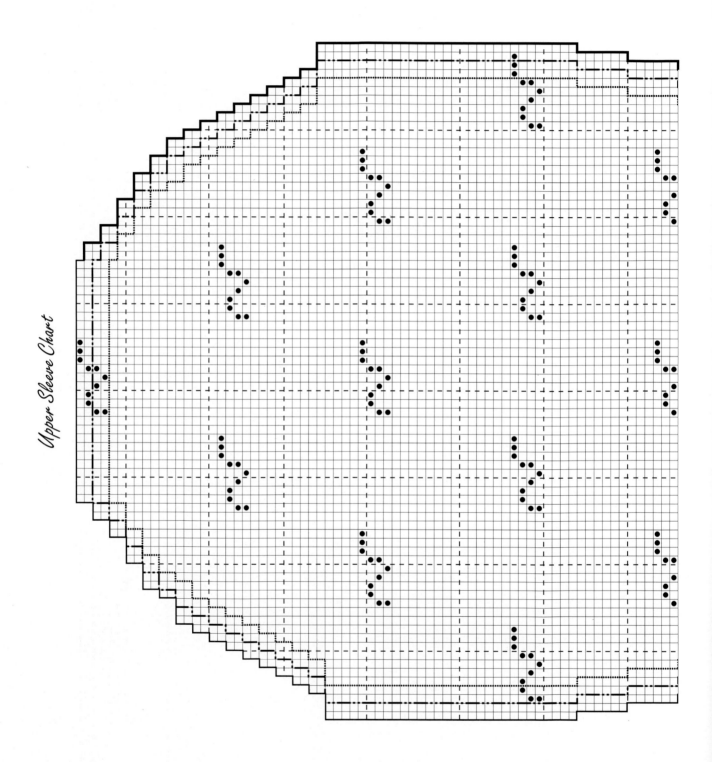

Lower Sleeve Chart

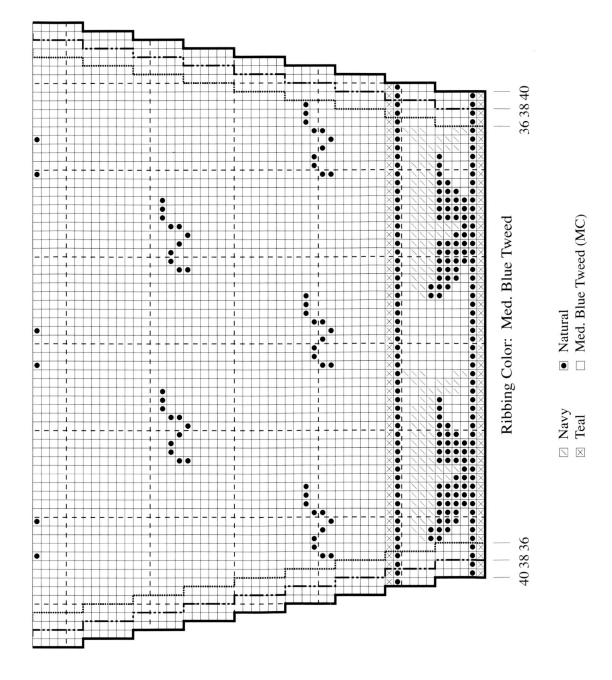

Ribbing Color: Med. Blue Tweed

☑ Navy   ◉ Natural
☒ Teal   ☐ Med. Blue Tweed (MC)

Foxberry

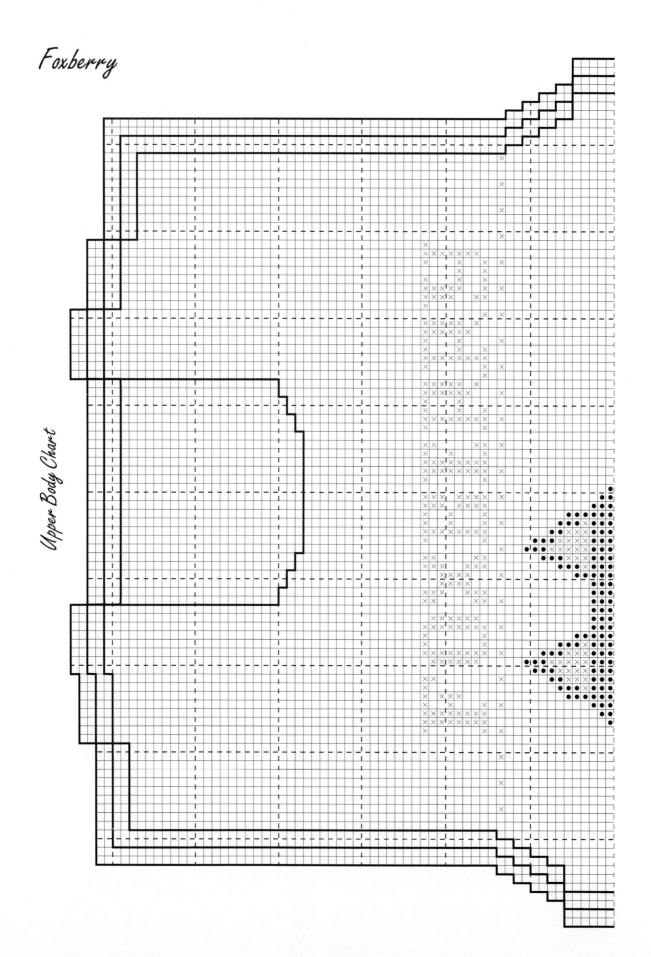

Upper Body Chart

Lower Body Chart

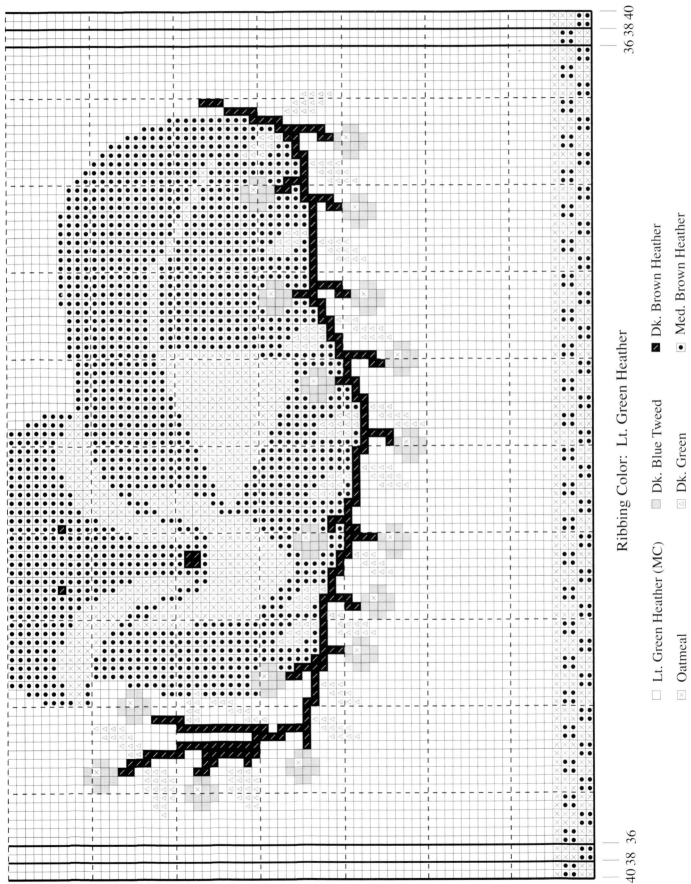

36 38 40

Ribbing Color: Lt. Green Heather

☐ Lt. Green Heather (MC)   ▨ Dk. Blue Tweed   ◪ Dk. Brown Heather

⊠ Oatmeal   ◩ Dk. Green   ● Med. Brown Heather

40 38 36

Foxberry

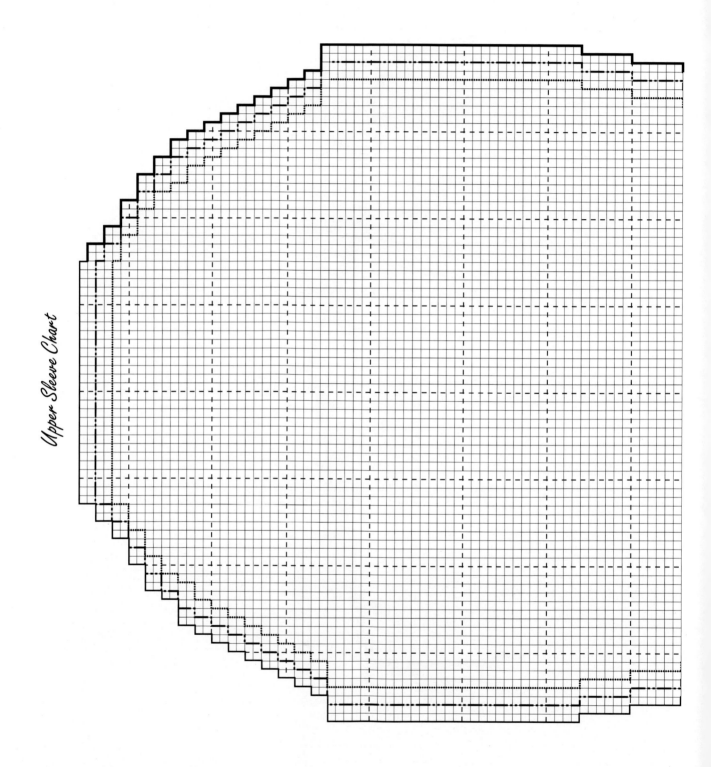

Upper Sleeve Chart

Lower Sleeve Chart

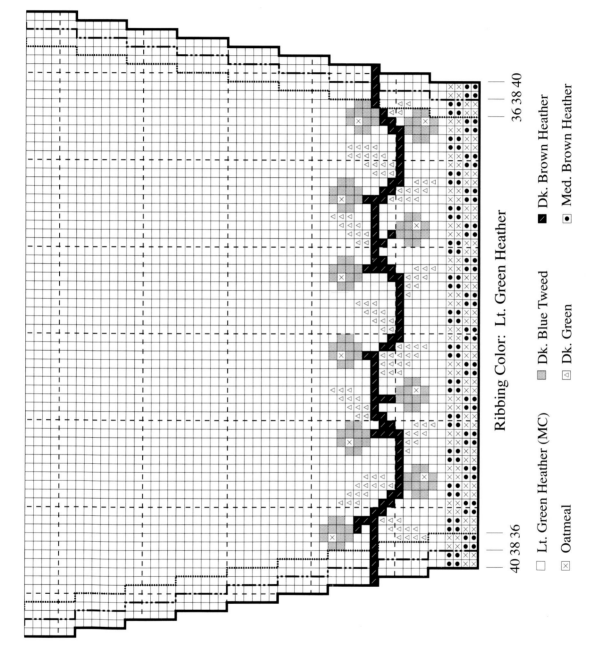

40 38 36

36 38 40

Ribbing Color: Lt. Green Heather

| | Lt. Green Heather (MC) | ■ | Dk. Blue Tweed | ■ | Dk. Brown Heather |
| | Oatmeal | ◁ | Dk. Green | ⊡ | Med. Brown Heather |

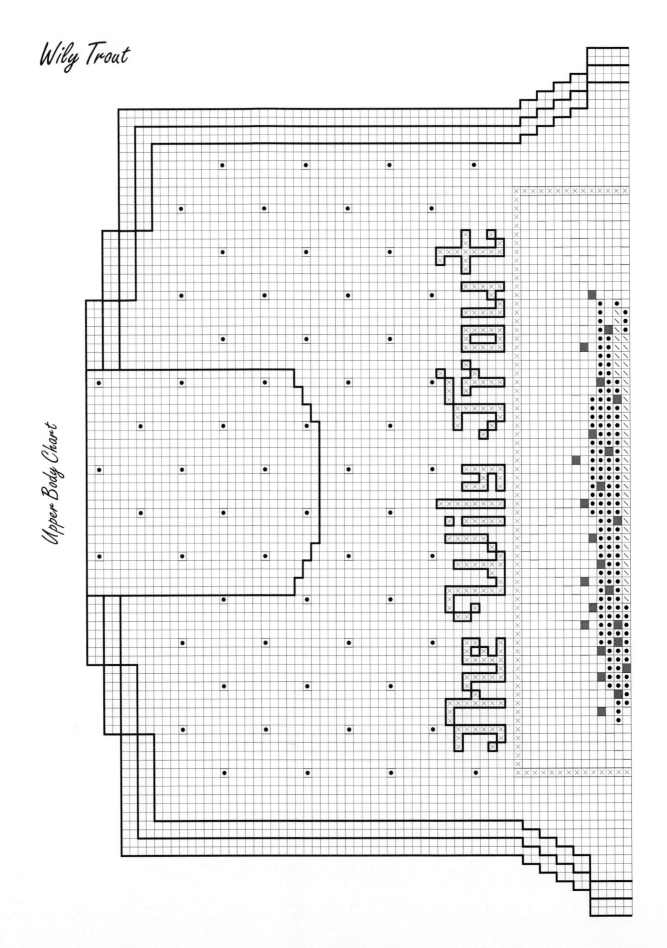

Upper Body Chart

Lower Body Chart

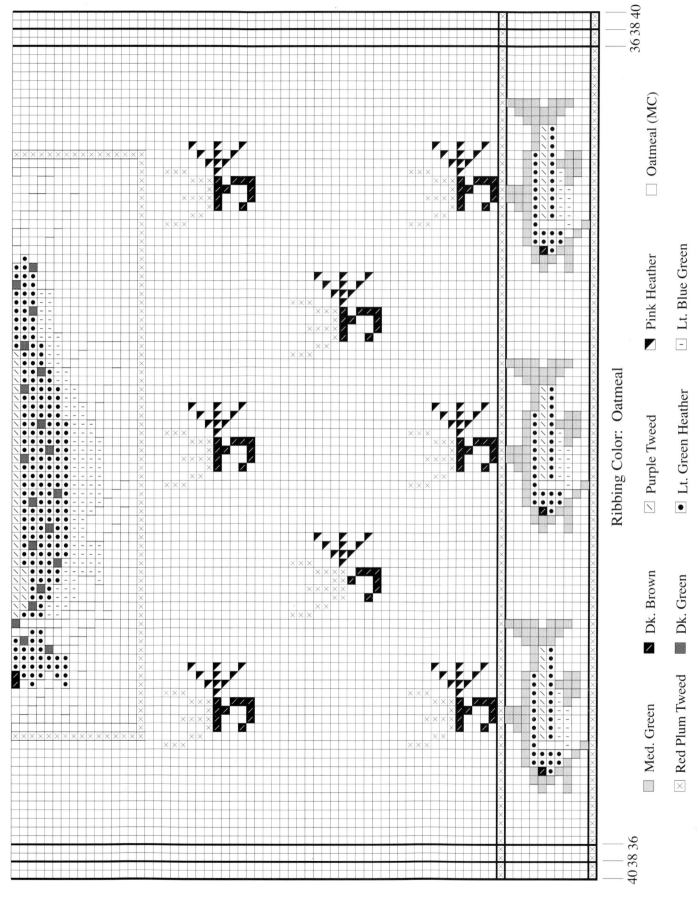

36 38 40

Ribbing Color: Oatmeal

40 38 36

	Med. Green		Dk. Brown		Pink Heather		Oatmeal (MC)
	Red Plum Tweed		Dk. Green		Purple Tweed		Lt. Blue Green
					Lt. Green Heather		

Wily Trout

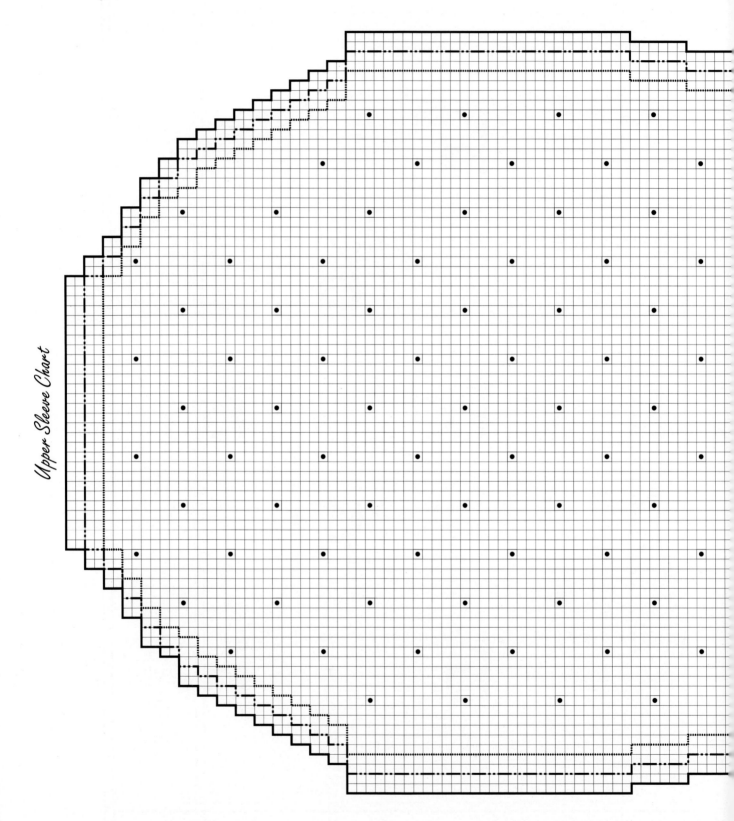

Upper Sleeve Chart

Lower Sleeve Chart

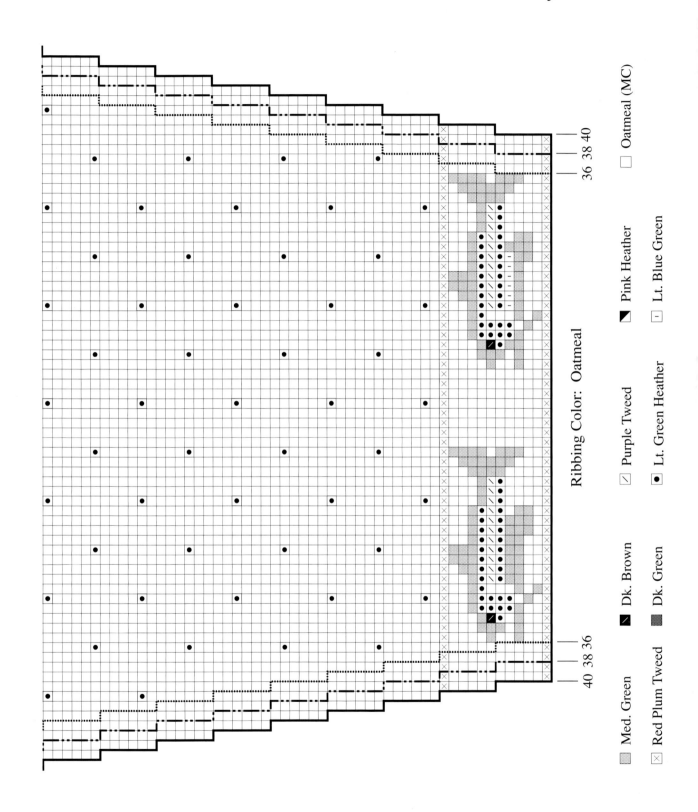

Ribbing Color: Oatmeal

| | Med. Green | ◼ | Dk. Brown | ◪ | Purple Tweed | ◣ | Pink Heather | ☐ | Oatmeal (MC) |
| | Red Plum Tweed | ◼ | Dk. Green | ● | Lt. Green Heather | – | Lt. Blue Green | | |

36 38 40

40 38 36

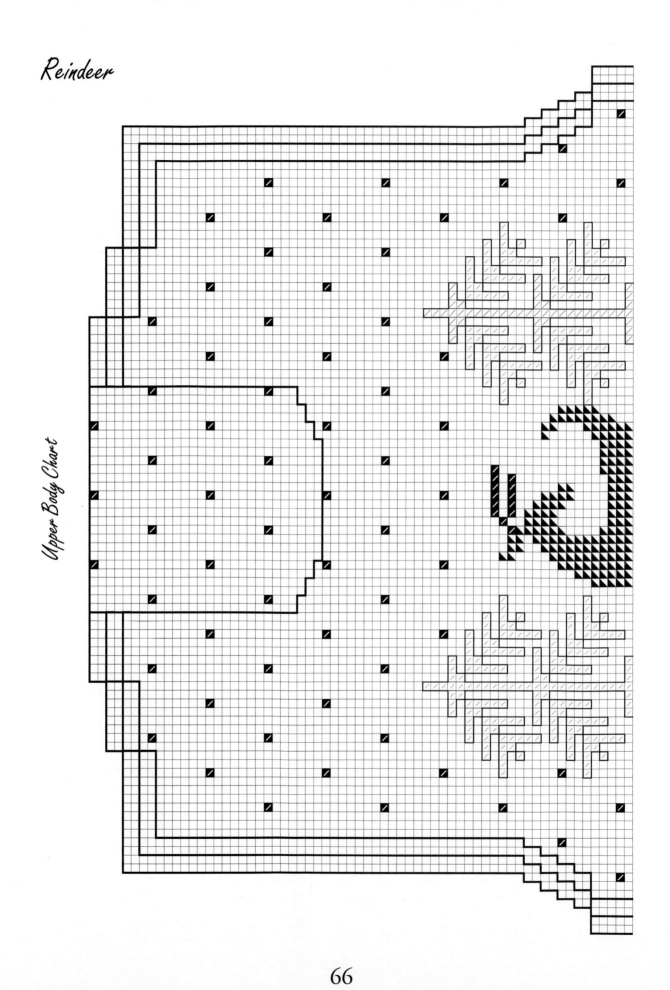

Lower Body Chart

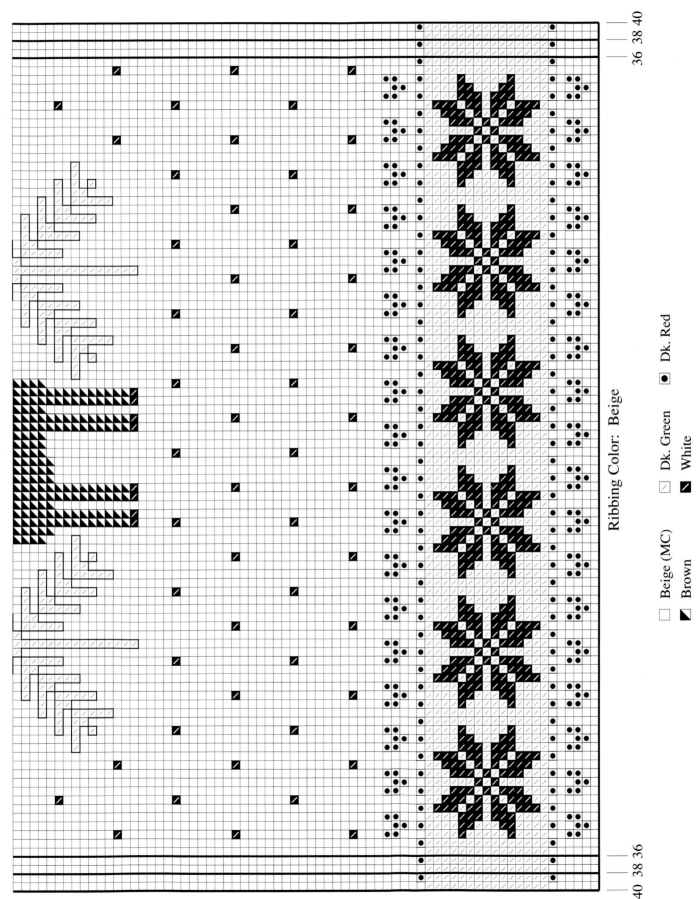

36 38 40
36 40
38 38 40

40 38 36

Ribbing Color: Beige

☐ Beige (MC) ⧄ Dk. Green ◉ Dk. Red
◤ Brown ◩ White

67

Reindeer

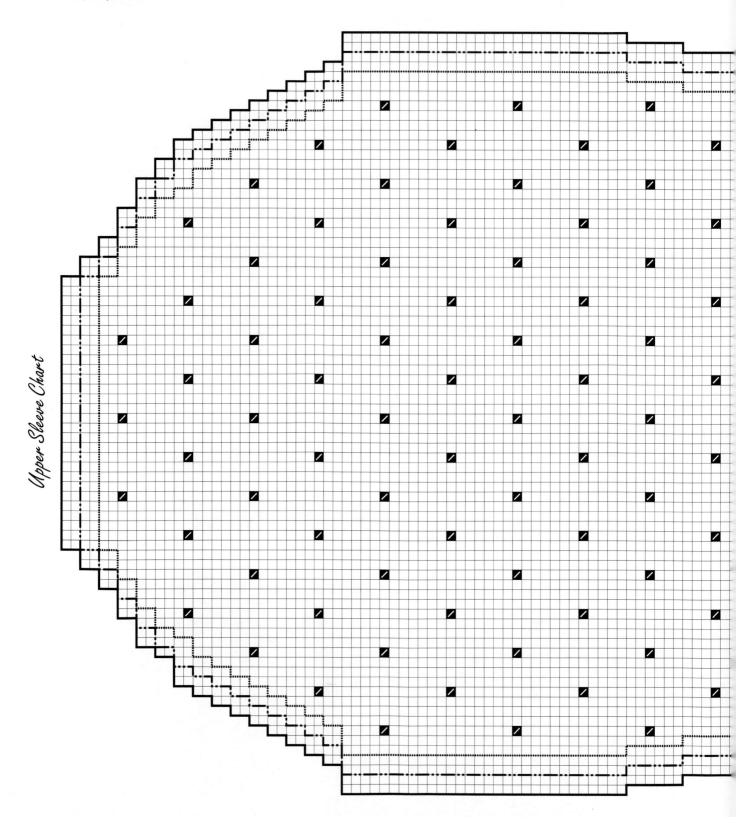

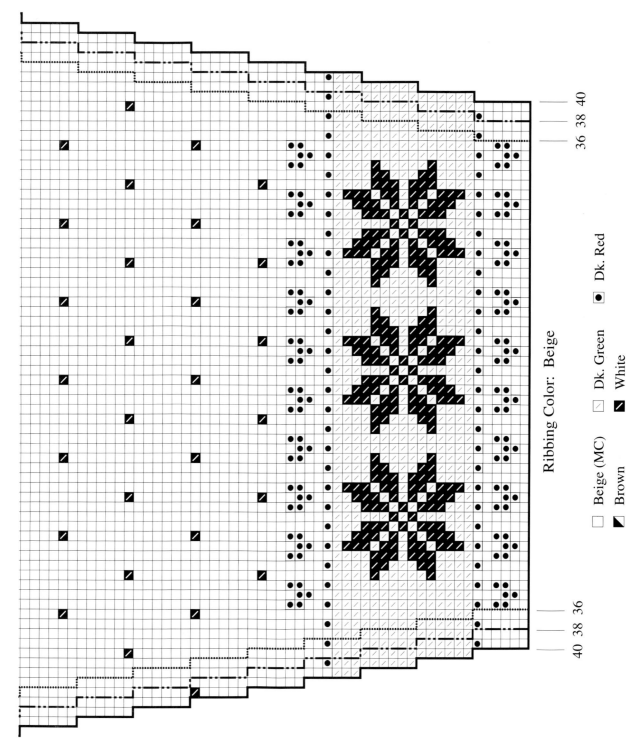

Lower Sleeve Chart

36 38 40

40 38 36

Ribbing Color: Beige

| ☐ Beige (MC) | ▨ Dk. Green | ● Dk. Red |
| ▨ Brown | ▨ White | |

Upper Body Chart

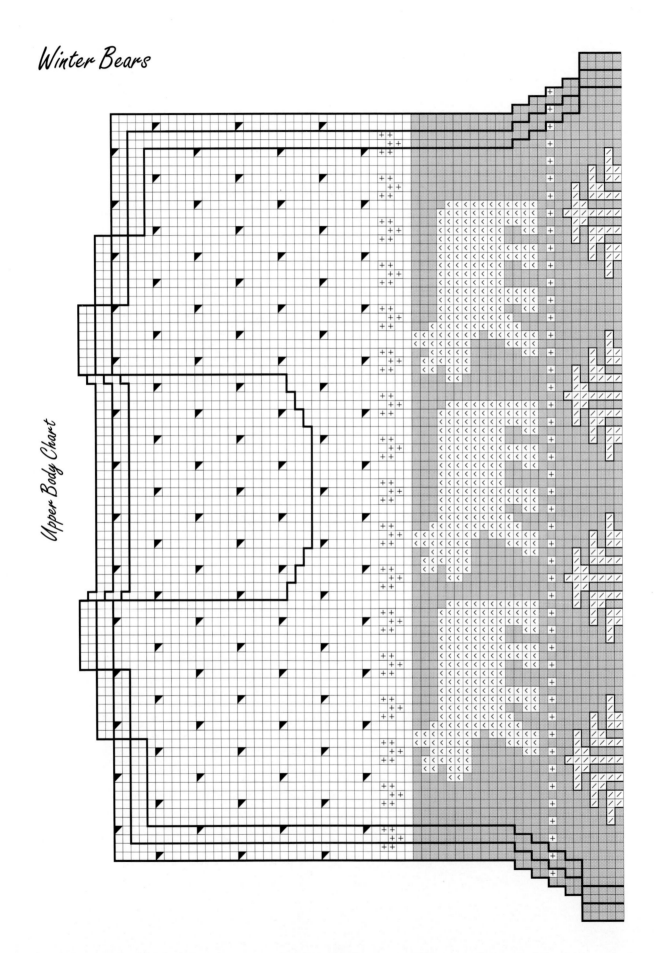

Lower Body Chart

36 38 40

40 38 36

Ribbing Color: Blue Gray

| | Blue Gray (MC) | | ☑ Dk. Green Heather | | ▨ Oatmeal | | ➕ Maroon Heather |
| ☒ Dk. Brown | | ⬛ Natural | | ● Med. Brown Heather |

71

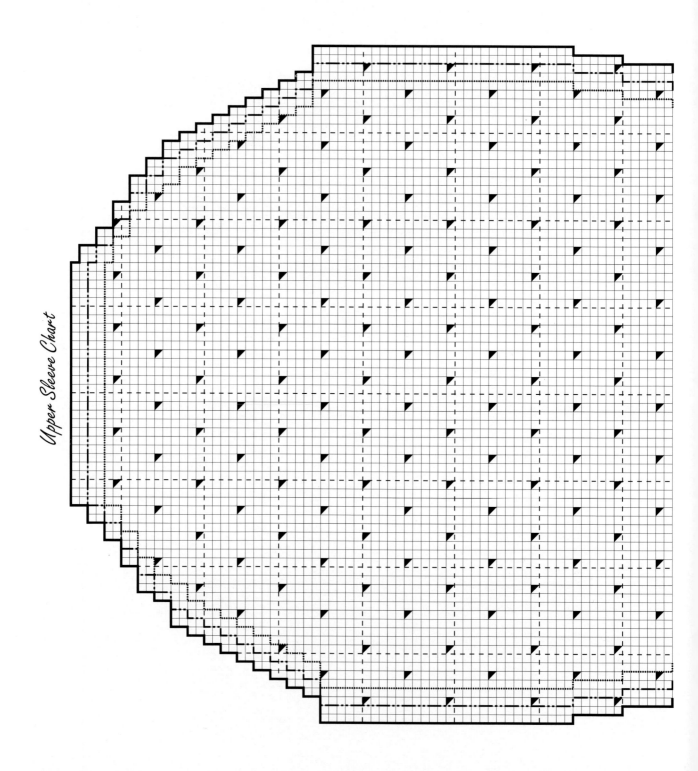

Upper Sleeve Chart

Lower Sleeve Chart

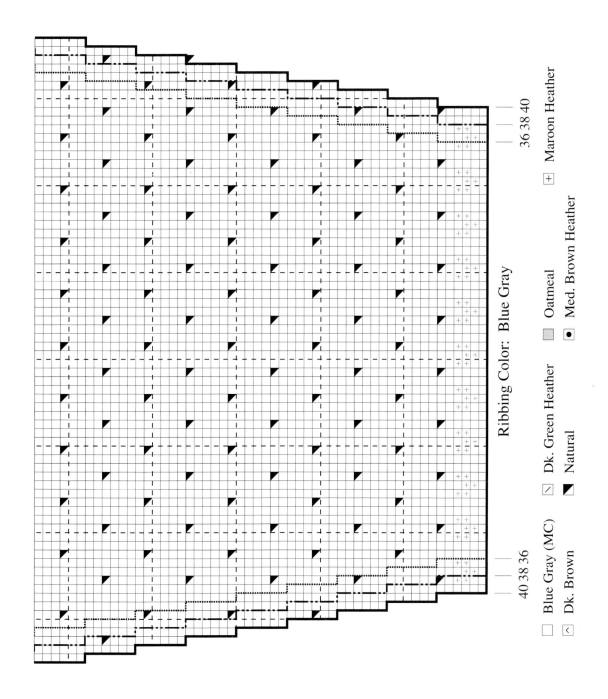

Ribbing Color: Blue Gray

| | Blue Gray (MC) | | Dk. Green Heather | | Oatmeal | | Maroon Heather |
| | Dk. Brown | | Natural | | Med. Brown Heather | | |

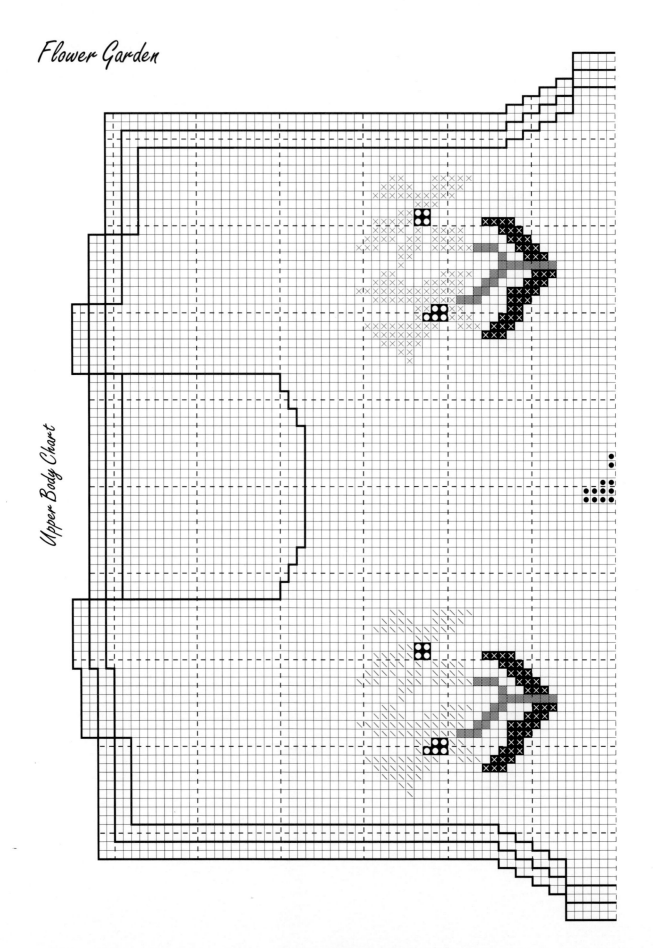

Upper Body Chart

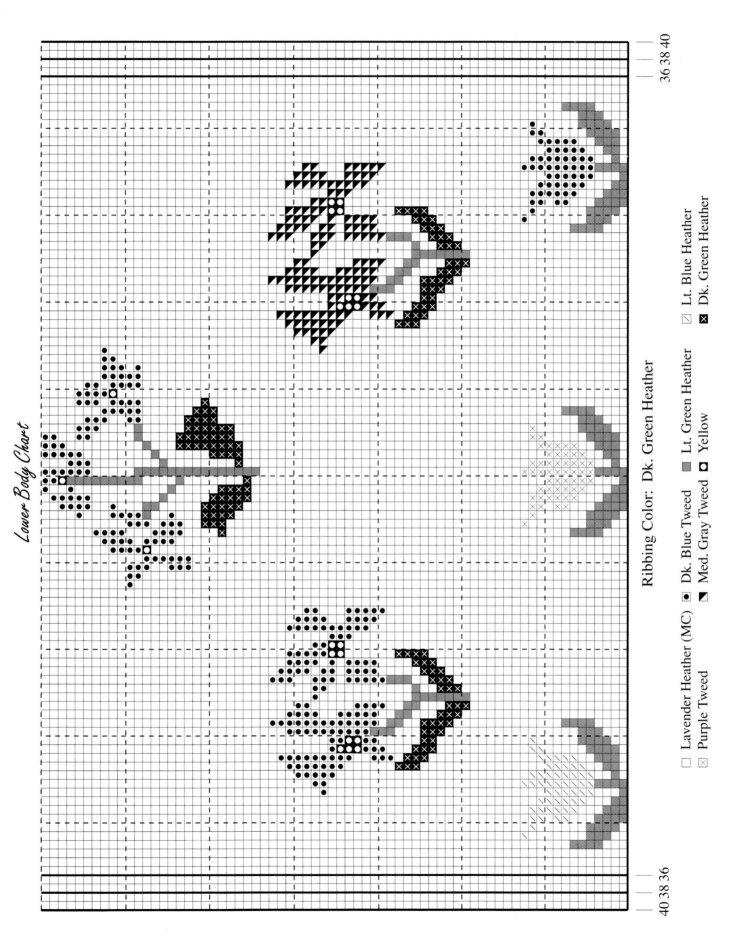

Lower Body Chart

36 38 40

40 38 36

Ribbing Color: Dk. Green Heather

☐ Lavender Heather (MC)   ● Dk. Blue Tweed   ▨ Lt. Green Heather   ☑ Lt. Blue Heather
☒ Purple Tweed   ◼ Med. Gray Tweed   ☐ Yellow   ☒ Dk. Green Heather

Flower Garden

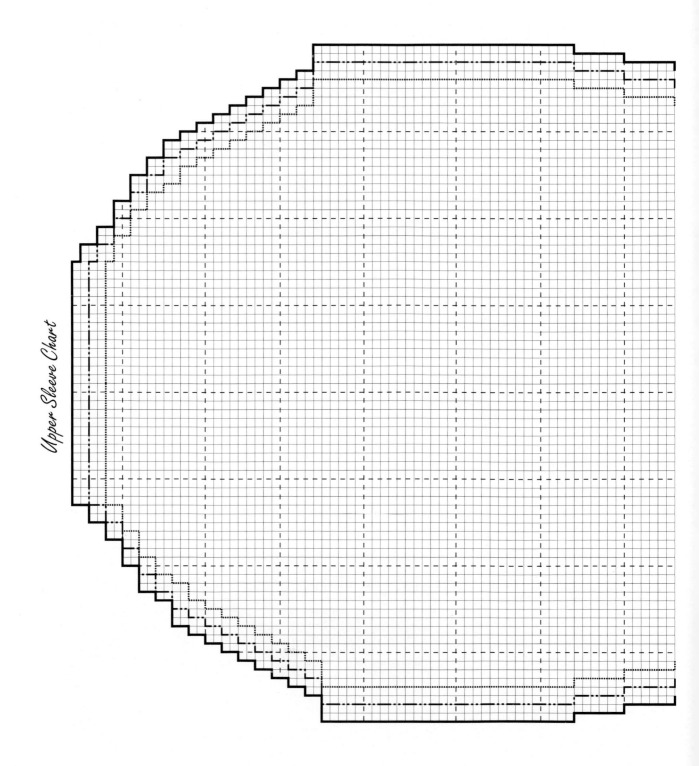

Upper Sleeve Chart

Flower Garden

Lower Sleeve Chart

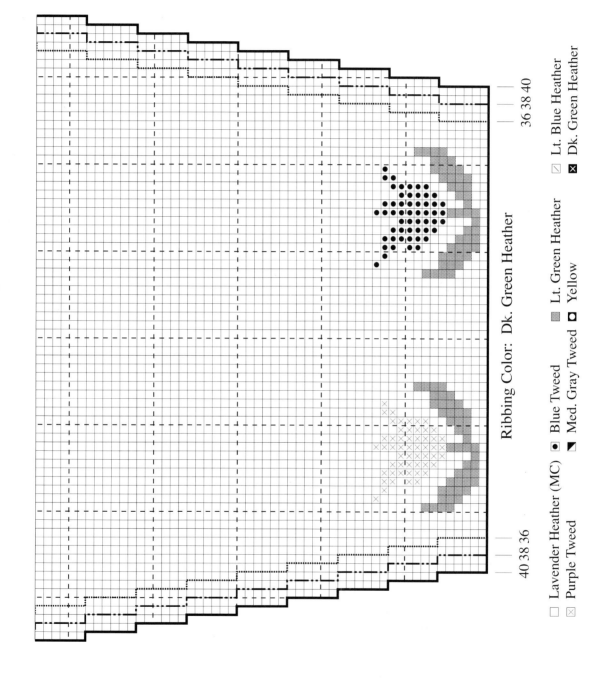

36 38 40

40 38 36

Ribbing Color: Dk. Green Heather

☐ Lavender Heather (MC)   ● Blue Tweed   ☒ Lt. Green Heather   ☐ Lt. Blue Heather
☒ Purple Tweed   ▦ Med. Gray Tweed   ☐ Yellow   ☒ Dk. Green Heather

Upper Body Chart

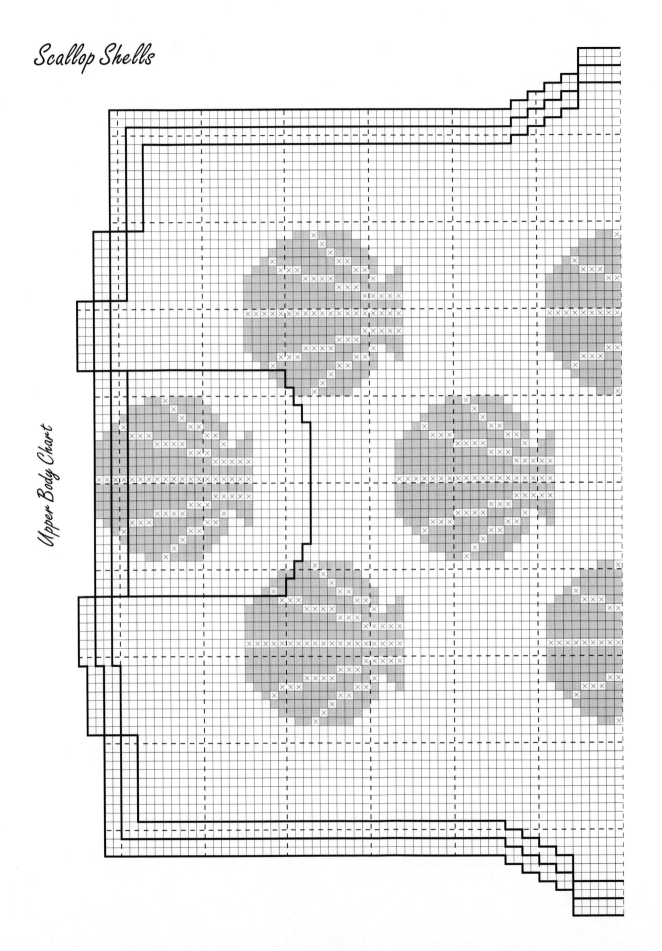

Lower Body Chart

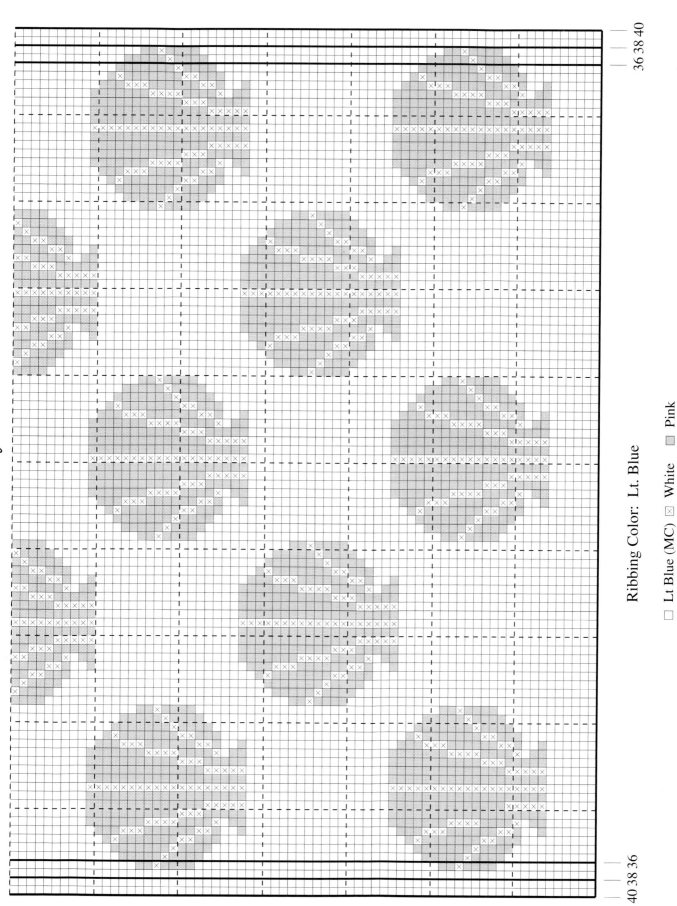

36 38 40

40 38 36

Ribbing Color: Lt. Blue

☐ Lt Blue (MC)   ☒ White   ▨ Pink

Scallop Shells

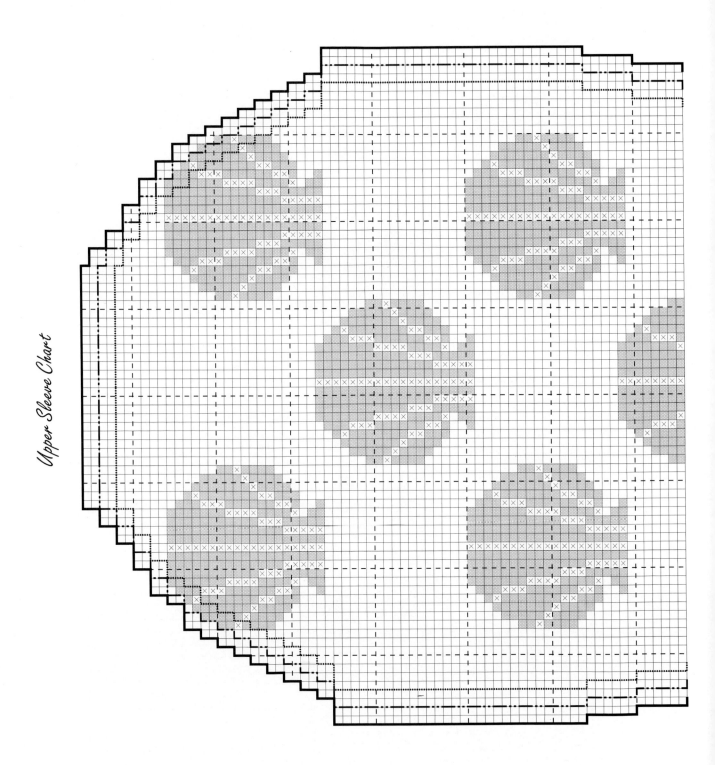

Upper Sleeve Chart

Lower Sleeve Chart

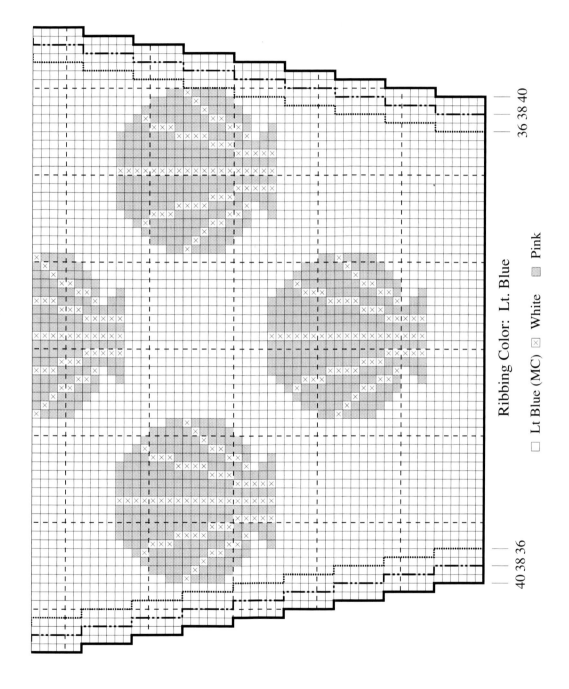

36 38 40

40 38 36

Ribbing Color: Lt. Blue

☐ Lt Blue (MC) ☒ White ▨ Pink

81

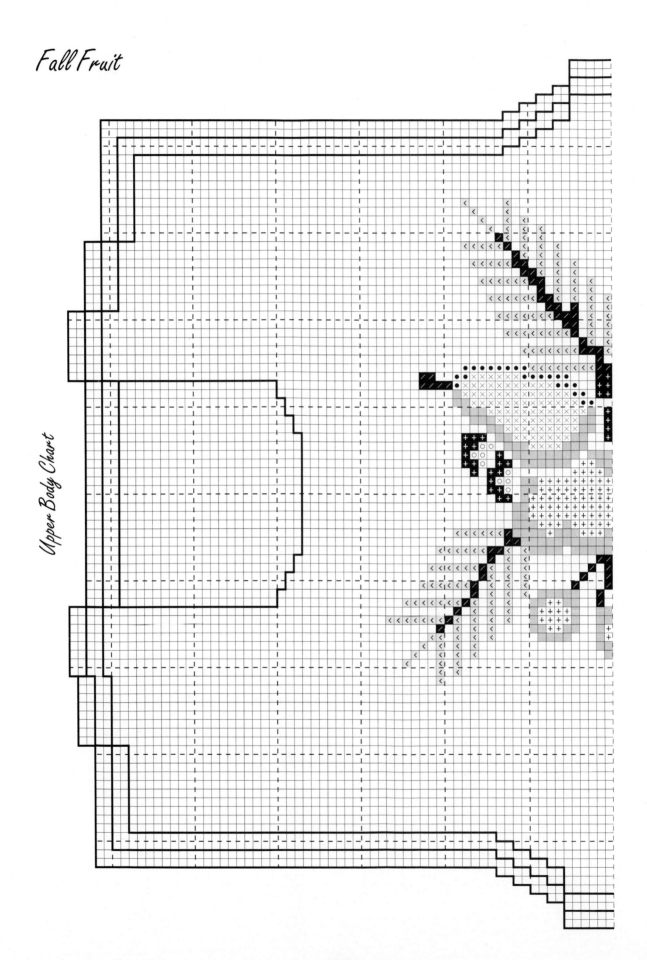

Upper Body Chart

Lower Body Chart

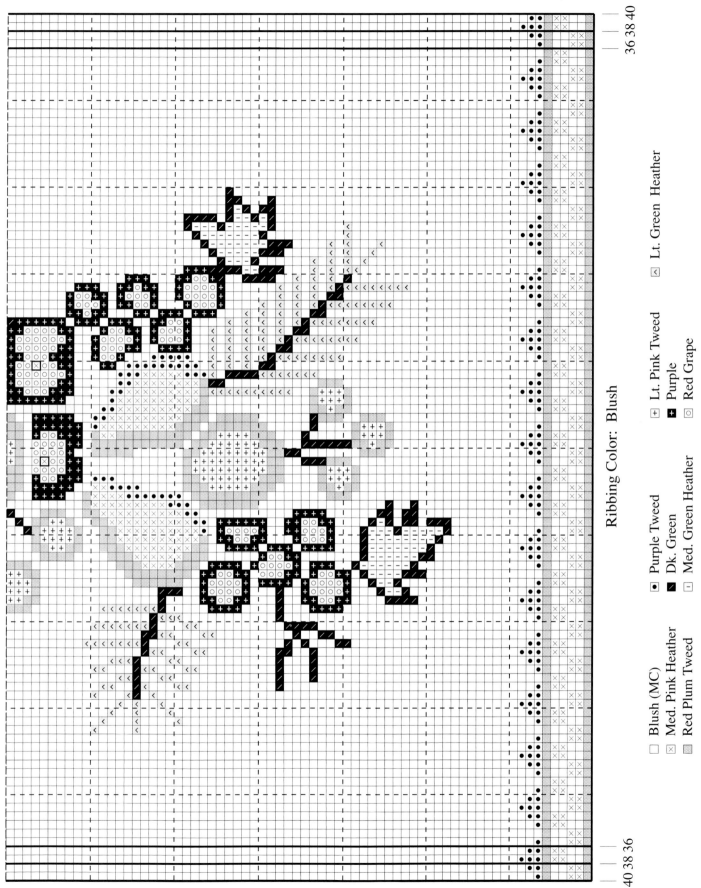

36 38 40

40 38 36

Ribbing Color: Blush

☐ Blush (MC)	⊡ Purple Tweed	⊞ Lt. Pink Tweed	⊠ Lt. Green Heather
⊠ Med. Pink Heather	■ Dk. Green	✚ Purple	
▨ Red Plum Tweed	⊡ Med. Green Heather	⊙ Red Grape	

83

Fall Fruit

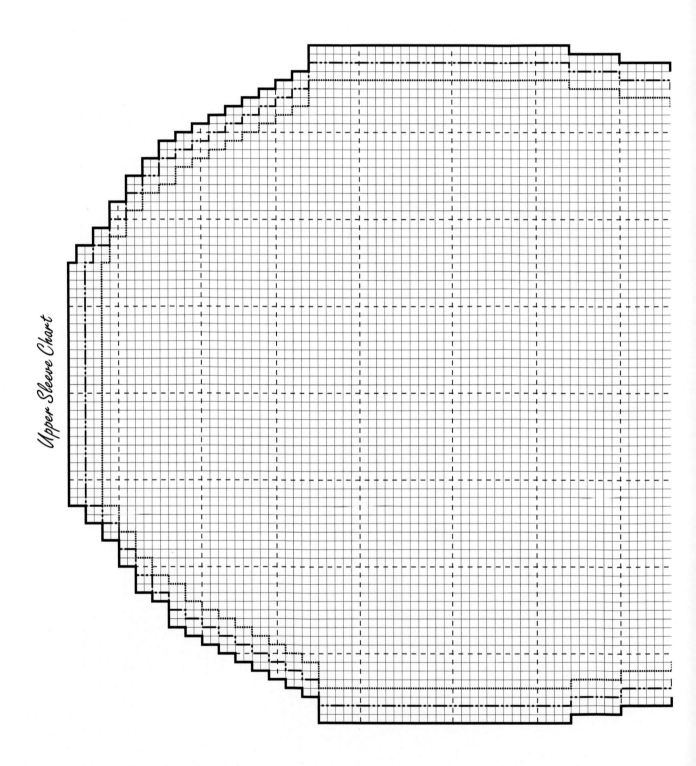

Upper Sleeve Chart

Lower Sleeve Chart

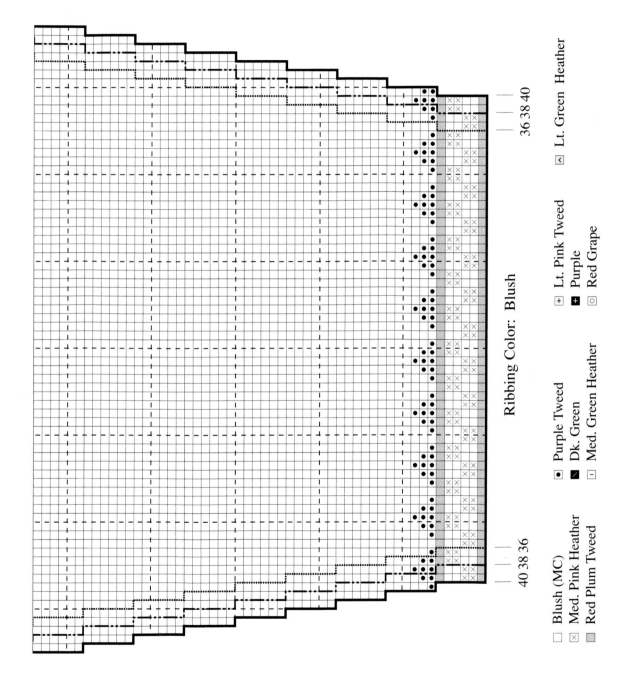

36 38 40

40 38 36

Ribbing Color: Blush

☐ Blush (MC)   ⊡ Purple Tweed   ⊞ Lt. Pink Tweed   ⊡ Lt. Green Heather
⊠ Med. Pink Heather   ◼ Dk. Green   ⊞ Purple
▨ Red Plum Tweed   ⊡ Med. Green Heather   ⊙ Red Grape

85

Upper Body Chart

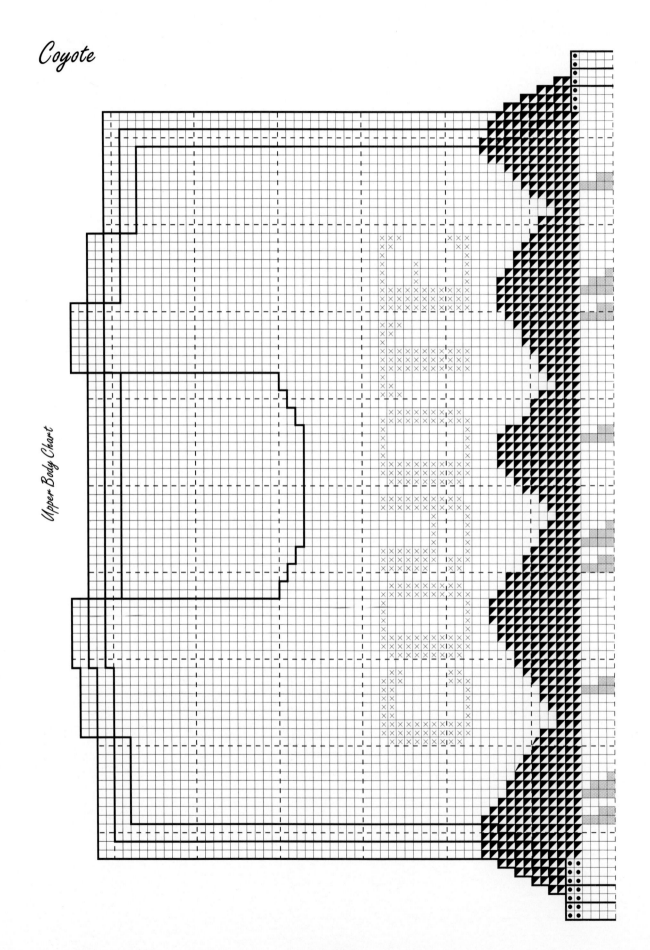

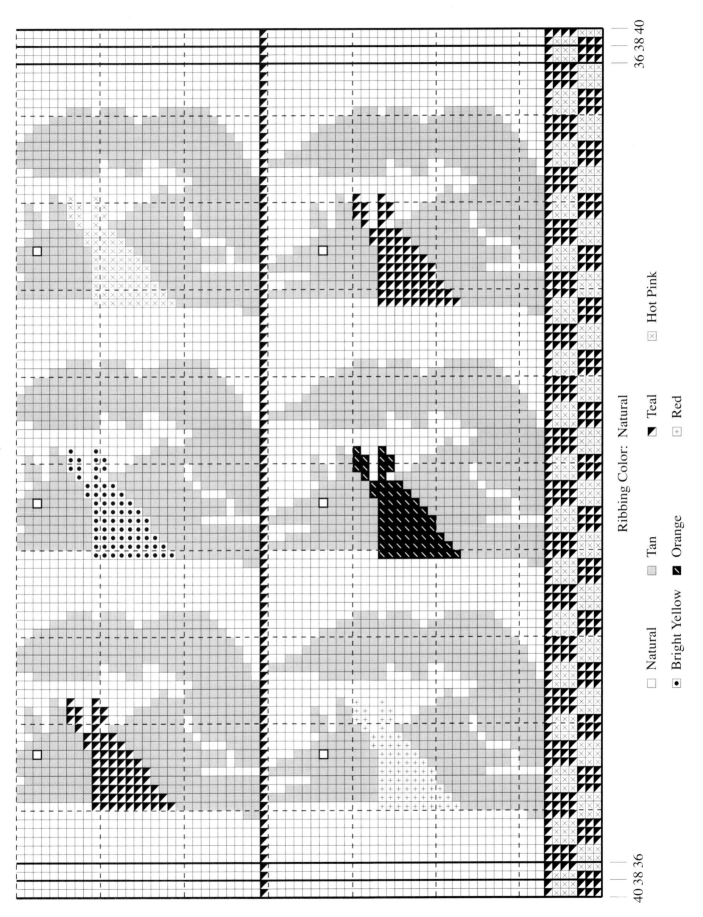

Lower Body Chart

36 38 40

40 38 36

Ribbing Color: Natural

☐ Natural	▨ Tan	◪ Teal	⊠ Hot Pink
• Bright Yellow	◪ Orange	⊞ Red	

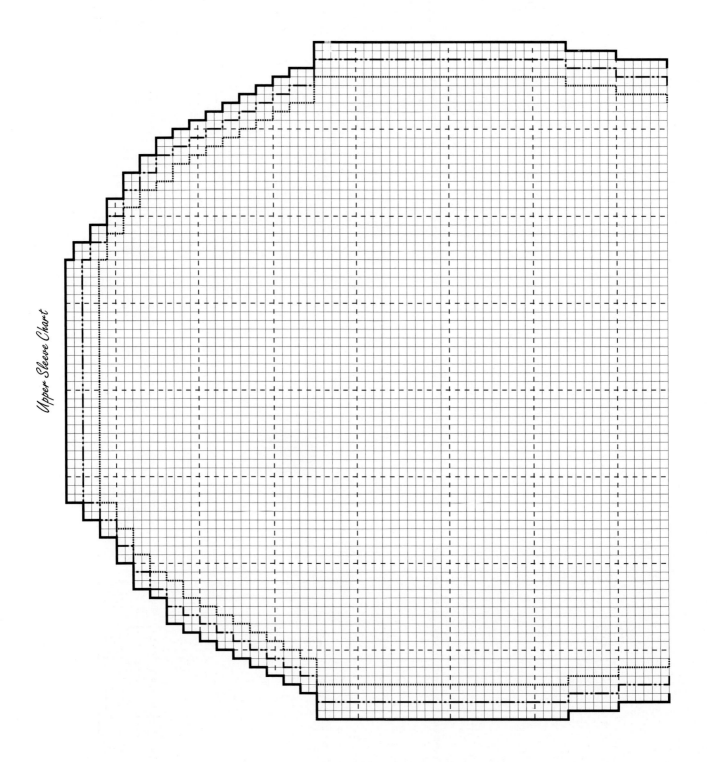

Upper Sleeve Chart

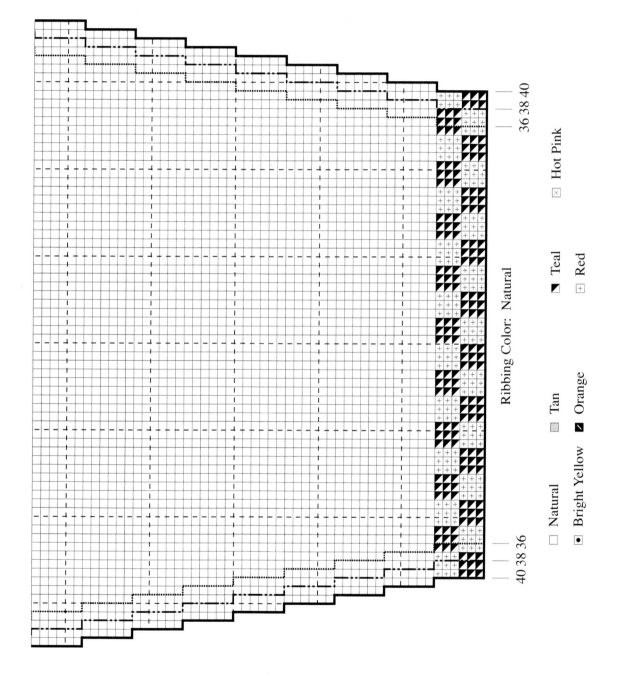

Lower Sleeve Chart

Ribbing Color: Natural

Natural   Tan   Teal   Hot Pink

Bright Yellow   Orange   Red

36 38 40

40 38 36

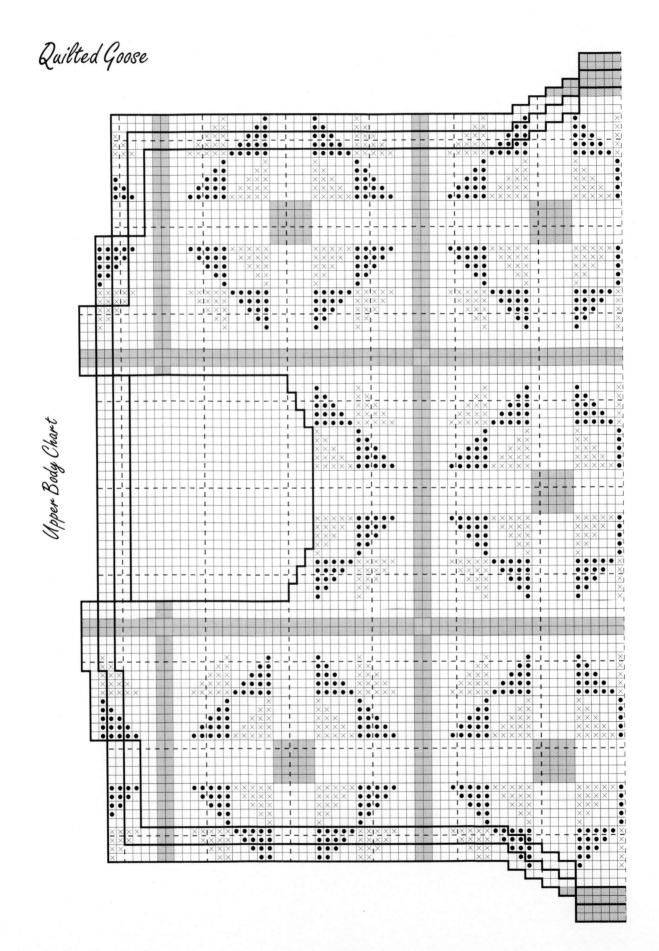

Upper Body Chart

Lower Body Chart

36 38 40

40 38 36

Ribbing Color: Dk. Blue Tweed

☐ Natural (MC)   ▦ Dk. Blue Tweed   ⊞ Gray Brown   ⊡ Dk. Green Heather
☒ Lt. Blue Green   ◉ Lt. Gray   ⊠ Black

Quilted Goose

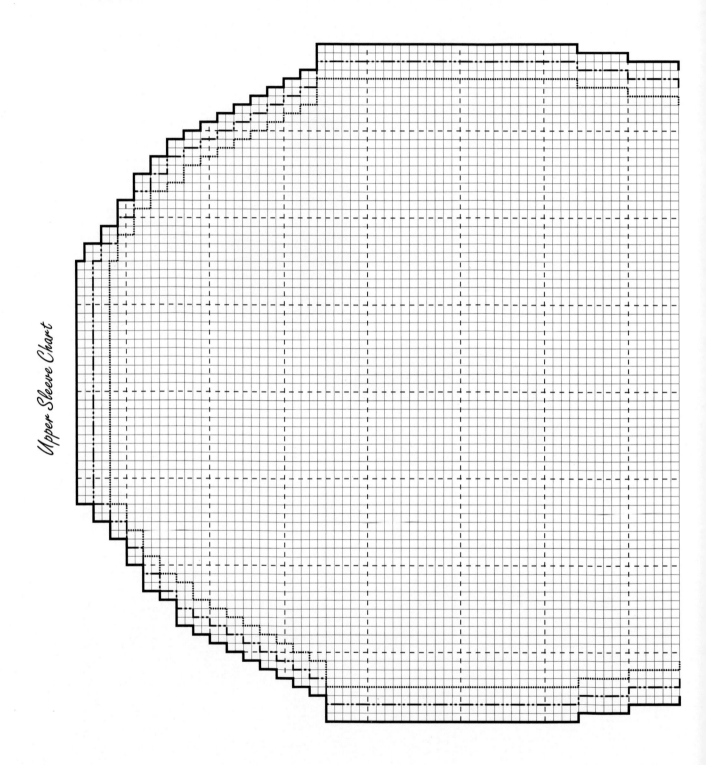

Upper Sleeve Chart

Lower Sleeve Chart

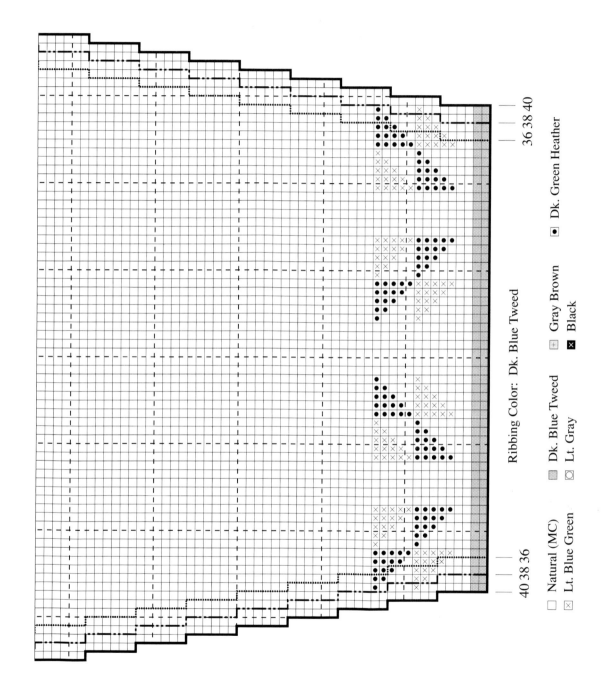

36 38 40

40 38 36

Ribbing Color: Dk. Blue Tweed

| ☐ Natural (MC) | ⊞ Dk. Blue Tweed | ⊞ Gray Brown | ⊡ Dk. Green Heather |
| ☒ Lt. Blue Green | ◙ Lt. Gray | ☒ Black | |

About Our Models

As with all of our knitting books, we asked our friends and neighbors to pose for these photos and depended on the great work of Peter Ralston to coax out the beauty that is present in every face. If you own any of our other books, many of the models in this one will look familiar—a child now being photographed as an adult, or a woman with another wrinkle of wisdom added to her face.

Kathy worked hard on the patterns in this book and also agreed to be photographed in one that she knit (page 10). She is a dedicated knitter who has helped the company in many ways through knitting samples, drafting patterns, and helping out in the office. Kathy was born on the island and recently returned after spending several years on the mainland living many places and getting a college degree. Her husband is the island minister, and her two sons attend our very small school.

Wendy (page 19), is one of the eleven children of the Cooper family, and like all of her siblings, she can be seen around town wearing many hats. She is a Special Education aide in our school, a peewee basketball coach, and manager of the videoshop/laundromat.

Allison, page 14, a very photogenic model, has consented to this grueling process several times, and we are always very grateful for her patience and wonderful smile. The mother of three young children, she moved to the island after years of sailing in the Caribbean and no doubt misses it during some of our long winter days.

We caught up with Laura (page 16) while she was visiting the Hallowells—the family of models we have come to depend on for many of our books. She is the waterfront reporter for a nearby coastal newspaper and has the enviable job of spending her days near the water rather than sitting at a desk.

Christie, our most frequently photographed model (remember the Lupine design in *Sweaters from the Maine Islands*?) stepped in for a brief shot in the Foxberry sweater on page 17. Christie lives on a beautiful small harbor with a nice garden, a few sheep, and her husband, the principal of our school.

My daughter Hannah makes an appearance in the Foxhunt sweater (page 12), looking a few years older than she did in *Maine Island Kids*. She is about to be a junior in high school and is anxiously looking forward to the day she can drive a car. Monica, her good friend, has turned out to be a loyal and photogenic model. She appears in the Sailboat sweater on page 15 (a fitting design as Monica begins her first summer as a sailing instructor).

Caroline, on page 22, was visiting the area from an island with far different characteristics from ours—Manhattan. We also managed to get two other women involved this year who do not live on the island but who have spent some time here. Robin (page 21) and Paula (on page 25) are hard-working staff members for the Island Institute, an organization dedicated to keeping islands and their year-round communities active, healthy, and beautiful places. They all made great models, and we appreciated their help.

Sources of Supply

As you can see from our earlier suggestions, we have a clear bias for natural materials. You may also want to try knitting one of these sweaters in more exotic yarns—raw silk, alpaca, angora, whatever your imagination dictates.

When looking for your materials, we suggest you search out your local yarn shop, and avoid your local discount department store. The yarn shop owner will likely be a knowledgeable knitter who can help you in making yarn decisions and will be there when you run into difficult times. Such shops will likely have many wonderful yarns for you to choose from. They are most likely also struggling small businesses in need of your support—you'll never know how much you depend on them until they are gone.

If you do not have a good local source for the materials to make the sweaters in this book, they are all available through us. We sell kits, skeined yarns, and yarn packs (all of the yarns needed to create one of these designs, packaged together in just the right quantities). We also produce a catalog that includes many knitting kits not featured in this book, as well as accessories such as buttons and wooden knitting needles. You can call us toll free to place an order, add your name to our mailing list or to ask a knitting question about our patterns. We'll keep you updated on our new designs and stories of island life.

North Island Designs
Main Street
North Haven, ME 04853
1-800-548-5648 (U.S. & Canada)
207-867-4788 (Maine)

Other Suppliers Include:

For 100% wool, fisherman-type yarns
Bartlettyarns, Inc.
Harmony, ME 04942
207-683-2251
They sell directly through the mail or can let you know the nearest retailer carrying their product.

Briggs & Little Woolen Mills, Ltd.
Harvey Station
York Mills, NB Canada EOH 1HO
506-366-5438
Sell direct as well as through retailers in this country.

For Lamb's Pride (85% wool, 15% mohair)
Brown Sheep Co.
Route 1
Mitchell, Nebraska 69357
1-800-826-9136
They can tell you your nearest dealer.